HAUNTED
SOUTHAMPTON

HAUNTED SOUTHAMPTON

Penny Legg

For Duncan, with love

First published 2011

The History Press
The Mill, Brimscombe Port
Stroud, Gloucestershire, GL5 2QG
www.thehistorypress.co.uk

ISBN 978 0 7524 5519 8

Typesetting and origination by The History Press
Manufacturing managed by Jellyfish Print Solutions Ltd.
Printed in India

Contents

Foreword

The Southampton area is rich in reported ghosts and ghostly happenings and we are fortunate to have Penny Legg as our guide in this haunted realm. She has explored the curious and the unexplained, the startling, the odd and the incredible stories associated with a wide variety of places. Private houses, public houses, historic buildings, railway stations and hospitals all are grist to her mill, and with a light but determined touch she recounts, often first-hand through the words of the witness concerned, some truly remarkable stories.

The investigation and study of paranormal happenings is always fascinating. The people involved are diverse and vary from the mundane to the eccentric while the stories one hears vary from the fantastic to the plausible. The responsibility of the chronicler is to differentiate between the highly improbable and the just possible, and to weigh up whether the stories are genuine or ingenious. Penny Legg has accomplished this admirably and here we have fair and balanced accounts of what might well have happened, together with the original sources.

We are indebted to the author and applaud her for casting her net wide in producing a book with lasting appeal. This is a book that will appeal to those who want the facts about the ghosts of Southampton; to those who would like to visit the haunted places of Southampton; those who accept the possibility of ghostly activity; and, perhaps especially, to those who have no knowledge of Southampton's ghost population.

This book has brought back to me the many happy hours that I spent hunting for ghosts in the Southampton area. It is a well-illustrated and thoughtful volume and cannot fail to be of interest to the general reader, the armchair ghost hunter or the serious parapsychologist. Entertaining and informative at the same time, I am delighted to recommend this book.

Here are to be found many previously unrecorded sightings of ghosts and ghostly activity in and around Southampton. Some of the interesting places you thought you knew you will find are haunted, and ghosts have been seen in many unlikely places so this book presents you with a new dimension for your visits and excursions. Where ghosts have once been seen, they may be seen again…

This is a valuable contribution to the literature of Southampton and its ghostly population.

Happy ghost hunting!

Peter Underwood, 2011

Acknowledgements

Many people have assisted with the research for this book. If I have missed your name from this list, I am sincerely sorry. I do thank you for your help:

Richard Ashman – Southampton Library Service; Sharron Baddams; Christine Bagg; Ross Bartlett; Ron Blatcher – New Zealand; Rob Butler; Gillian Clarke, Footner & Ewing Solicitors; Pete and Juliet Collins – Haunted Southampton Ltd; Lee Davies; Nicola Golding; Julie and Roger Green; David Hart; David Hollingworth – Southampton Local History Librarian; Alan House; Andrew House; Barry Kinceh; Merita King; Joe Legg; Kelly Leigh; James Marsh; Chris Mould; Joan Shergold; Barrie and Jo Short and the staff at The Old Farmhouse; Southern Paranormal UK; Adele Stevens – manager of The Station Pub, Bitterne; Hannah Tate; the members of the Haunted Southampton Ltd. Facebook site; TrueGhostTales.com; Peter Underwood; Nicola and Keith Venton – The Brushmaker's Arms, Upham; Sue Wardall; Pam Whittington; Nigel Wood.

All images are courtesy of the author unless stated otherwise.

About The Author

enny Legg was born in Surbiton. She moved to Southampton in 1998. She is a writer and photographer; she is also a former editor of *The Woman Writer* magazine for the Society of Women Writers and Journalists. She is fascinated by the paranormal, having lived in a haunted house herself. However, as she admits, it was only her grandmother, and various startled visitors, who saw the little girl dressed in Edwardian-style clothing who shared the house with her family. This book stems in part from Penny's research for chapter two of her recent book, *Folklore of Hampshire*. In her spare time, Penny is a PADI Master Scuba Diver, she loves to dance and she runs Writing Buddies, a group for writers in Southampton.

The author, Penny Legg. (Photograph by Rob Innis)

Introduction

I will always remember this book as the one that did not want to be written. Looking back at the events that happened while I was working on it, it seems as if some unseen force was in the background, tripping me up as I fought my way through to the end. This may sound fanciful and perhaps it is, but, when I think about, for example the dreadful cold I had one snowy January day, I do start to wonder. I went to meet Andrew House to talk about his paranormal investigation work, and felt fine when we started chatting. However, I became aware that something was creeping up on me as we talked and it made me sneeze so much it is a wonder I could ask him anything! Then the Dictaphone died... Sorry Andrew. I hope you did not pick up the germs I must have been spreading across half of Southampton!

It was the day that all the notes for this book, and much of the first draft, were stolen that had me in tears though. I had foolishly left my bag on the train on a visit to see my family and when I got the bag back, just thirty minutes later, the portable hard drive on which the book was saved, had gone. I hope whoever stole it is pleased with themselves. I had to put the book back together again almost from scratch, with the result that my beginning of June deadline became an August one. By the time I was coming to the end of my work on *Haunted Southampton*, I was also promoting my first book, *Folklore of Hampshire*, tidying up the photographs and approving the cover design of my next book, *Southampton: Then and Now,* and was working on my following book, *Winchester: History You Can See.* Time became very precious and there was never enough of it in a day. Added to that, my computer crashed just as I was putting the final draft together, and I lost some of the work I was busy on at the time, which had to be rewritten. *Haunted Southampton* seemed to take longer and longer to write and I thank my patient publisher for understanding.

I am indebted to several people for assistance with this book. They are all listed in the acknowledgements section, but there are certain people who deserve an extra mention. The first is my ever-patient husband, Joe, who dispenses much-needed hugs in times of stress and who is quite happy to go junketing about Southampton and its suburbs when I need to take photographs.

I was not sure how Peter Underwood would react if I asked him to write the Foreword for *Haunted Southampton*. I mean, he is a famous ghost hunter, prolific writer on the subject and much respected in his field. Who was I to make requests of him?

I was therefore absolutely delighted to receive his gracious letter of acceptance and my smile was radiant when I read the resulting piece. Thank you, Peter.

Juliet and Pete Collins of Haunted Southampton Ltd, the paranormal investigative company here in the city, gave me much time to ask questions and allowed me access to their Facebook pages to appeal for first-hand ghost stories for this book. This was a huge help to me and I would like to thank them, and Pete's brother, Pat, for granting me this assistance, and for making me very welcome on one of their enquiries.

The members of the Haunted Southampton Facebook site are a wonderful bunch and, although I could not use all of the stories I was offered in this book, I would like to thank everyone for their help and assistance. It was fascinating hearing your stories and learning to understand the experiences you have had.

I have dedicated this book to my brother Duncan, who has long been fascinated by ghosts, spirits, apparitions and other manifestations of the paranormal. I hope this book doesn't keep him awake at night!

What came across during my research for this book was just how many ghost stories there are in this area of Hampshire. Spirits seem to appear everywhere and are not just isolated occurrences. I hope you enjoy the tales I have uncovered.

Penny Legg, 2011

1

Around the City

Types of Paranormal Activity

Many of us know the strange shadows we catch sight of, out of the corner of our eye, as 'ghosts', or refer to paranormal activity as 'things that go bump in the night'. What are we really talking about though? The *Concise Oxford English Dictionary* states that a ghost is 'the supposed apparition of a dead person or animal; a disembodied spirit' but what exactly does this mean? Are there different types of haunting? Andrew House helpfully gives us a quick briefing on the different types of activity he has come across as a paranormal investigator. He starts though with a starling statistic: 'Seventy-six per cent of ghost reports are during the day, when we are about.' This would tend to contradict the 'bump in the night' theory! He says:

> Some ghosts are interactive, such as the repeat apparition, who replays an event over and over and cannot talk to mediums. Active spirits can be stuck in one room, these are called Landers, or stuck in one house, called Grounders. Elemental spirits are those who have never lived in a physical body. They cannot move anything. A poltergeist is a noisy ghost. They are not always nasty but they want to make contact with the living. They can move and touch.

It is the poltergeist that is perhaps the best known of the paranormal phenomena. The Amityville Horror story is a famous example of poltergeist activity, but as Andrew says, 'Nasty stories are always more newsworthy.'

Andrew explains different types of parananormal phenomena further:

> A Crisis Apparition occurs when someone wants to say a final farewell. This was common during the First and Second World Wars. A Doppelganger is a spirit who looks like someone you know and these are not often reported.
>
> Some spirits are Wanderers. Henry VIII is a famous wanderer. He is often associated with the Tower of London, the most haunted place in England. Dame Alicia Lisle is another famous

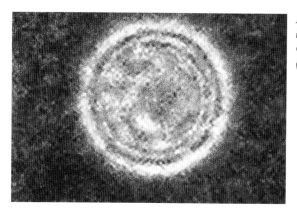

A close-up of an Orb. This shows the internal rings within the outer circle. This Orb was photographed in Portswood. (Photograph courtesy of Julie Green)

wanderer, a victim of 'Hanging Judge Jeffries'. She was executed after the Battle of Sedgemoor and is seen at the Eclipse Inn in Winchester – where she spent her last night and outside which she was hanged – and her home, Moyles Court in Ellingham, Hampshire.

A 'Grey Lady' is often seen and this is a full apparition, glimpsed in the shadows. Ghosts are a form of energy, of heat. They use energy to manifest. At séances they use the energy from those participating.

An Orb cannot be seen by the naked eye but can be caught on camera. This is both the first and last stage of a haunting.

An established theory in the paranormal world, although not a proven theory in the scientific one, is the stone tape theory, which states that brickwork has the quality to record events in time and then to replay them. As Andrew says, 'These are often castle-type buildings.'

As we shall read in the stories in this book, there are many different types of haunting active in Southampton today.

The Southampton City College

The children's nursery at the Southampton City College is built on the site of an old workhouse. The Southern Life website tells us that St Mary's workhouse was built there in 1774, the result of an endowment from John Major, the Mayor of Southampton, in 1629. The workhouse's original site was in French Street. A new workhouse was built, after a great deal of consultation, on the site in St Mary's Street, now owned by the City College, and its name was changed to the Union Workhouse. It was enlarged and, in 1881, held 240 adults, 100 boys and 110 girls. The building was replaced in 1886, the old premises being pulled down, and the new workhouse had room for over 500 paupers and two schools on the site.

Hannah Tate knew there was something funny about the place when she went there for an interview for a job at the nursery two years ago. 'I tend to pick up feelings a lot more than anyone else.' She continues:

It was just the sense that something felt a bit odd when I went for the interview. It's a nursery so there were lots of children running around. It is a happy, chirpy kind of place but something felt off. About a week after I started, one of my colleagues asked me to come outside with her; she hated being in the building by herself because apparently there were reports of things that had scared her. So, at that point, it was a relief to know it was not just me and there were actually things behind it.

Unexplained sightings of people are common in the corridors at the nursery:

I have a work mate who, when she is on an early shift at seven in the morning, has to unlock everything. She said that she would hear singing or footsteps behind her, following her in the corridor and, at one point she looked into the glass of a fire door and saw the face of a young boy looking back at her from the other side. There was nobody there though as no one was in the building at the time. I have had different experiences there, too. Not too long after I first started, it was early evening and I was doing some washing up after the children had had their dinner. They were all on the other side of the room to me and I felt a tapping on my trouser leg, as if one of the children wanted my attention, and so I looked down but no one was there.

Other reported strange occurrences have included staff hearing their names being called but receiving blank looks from colleagues when they responded:

One day I was walking down towards the kitchen, and, as I turned the corner to go down the corridor where the kitchen is, I thought I saw somebody going into it. I didn't think anything of it, so I carried on down the corridor, went into the kitchen and, no one was there! The only other door in there was out into the college itself and that door is always locked and it had a chair barring it. I must have been about 25ft away and so I only saw the person's back and heard the door closing. When I got into the kitchen I thought, hang on! I saw someone going in here, where are they?

There have also been reports of one of the girls going to get her bag after her shift and her actually seeing someone, fleetingly, up in the staff room, just as she opened the door to go in. There was no one there when she walked through it and went in.

Although the atmosphere in the old, original parts of the City College campus itself has been described as 'vague and dark', it seems that it is just the staff who see the unusual visitors to the nursery. Hannah and a friend thought that they would try an experiment to see if anything came of it. They placed a trigger object, a bucket, in the staff room when they finished a late shift on a Friday and were first in the building on the Monday morning. They were amazed to see that the bucket had moved an inch from the place they had placed it.

Hannah neatly sums up the case: 'Quite a few of the girls do get quite freaked out. They didn't mention that at the interview!'

Archer's Lodge

A story carried by the *Southern Daily Echo* dating from 3 August 1951 makes interesting reading.

It concerns the ghost of an Archer's Lodge resident. Archer's Lodge stood on the site later occupied by the Southampton Convent High School in The Avenue.

The story was printed in a Jesuit magazine, *Stella Maris*, and relates the sad tale of Philip Weld. Philip was the son of James Weld of Archer's Lodge and was the nephew of Cardinal Thomas Weld (1773 – 1837), a relative by marriage of Mrs Fitzherbert, (1756 – 1837) George IV's mistress.

In 1842 Philip was sent to school at St Edmund's College in Ware, Dorset. He was drowned while out rowing on the River Lea four years later. The president of the college, the Very Reverend Dr Cox decided to journey to Southampton to give the sad news to Philip's parents in person. As he was coming up The Avenue in his carriage he saw James Weld walking along the road towards the gates of Archer's Lodge. Dr Cox pulled up and got out of his carriage to speak to him. Before he could say a word, James Weld spoke, telling him that he knew why he had come.

Weld went on to explain that he and his daughter Katherine had been walking in The Avenue the day before and had seen Philip, dressed all in black, with two other people. 'Suddenly they all vanished and I saw nothing but a man whom I had seen through the three figures, which gave me the impression they were spirits.' Dr Cox's appearance was enough to confirm Weld's suspicion that his son was dead.

The Tudor House Museum

The UK Paranormal Society investigated the reports of strange happenings at the Tudor House Museum in the city centre. According to Andrew House, the company's owner, UK PRS was the first paranormal group to think the building was haunted.

Andrew takes up the story:

The City Council own the Tudor House Museum and have had ten years of reports of people having had strange experiences there; staff have left because something happened – people would see shadows, hear noises or see things that move and they would think, that is not quite right, and leave. They had a security guard who was actually working there when I was working on the case and he would not come into the house on his own. Once when he was alone setting the alarm he said he heard a door slam, a big heavy fire door, that couldn't physically close of its own accord. He said after that there was no way he was ever going into that house again.

The Tudor House Museum has houses around it and the police consistently get people who phone up and say they see someone in the Tudor House's window but that can't happen because the alarm would have gone off. Things happen all the time so we went in there over the course of a year because the Council said to us, 'Could you go in and see what is going on? We've had enough!' We went back during the day, during the evening and at different times of day as well, as we needed to see what was going on. I also spoke to people who worked there over the past thirty years and many of them came forward and said 'I've seen something', so I sat down with them and interviewed them to see what happened. What we found is that a lot of them, although they didn't know each other, were reporting similar things. What you realise is that if they don't know each other and there are no documented reports of ghostly incidences then there must be something strange going on because the people's experiences were consistent. So I took a note of all of the occurrences and then spent several nights in the house itself and took photos to see what would happen.

I saw several things, I have to say. We stayed one night in the cellar, which is actually a vault, where there is no natural light. The Council had left us with the keys for the night. I locked the doors so no one could physically come into that room. All of us saw someone walk across the room. We thought it was one of our team coming from somewhere and asked, 'What are you doing?' There was no one there. There was a bricked-up doorway where this person left the room, so nobody could physically have got out of that room. It was obviously a bricked-up doorway. The brickwork around it was still there. We either all imagined it or it was something paranormal. It was interesting and the Council was quite happy about that! They still use it on their tours now, as a story.

Upstairs, on the first floor in the old Tudor part, there were footsteps but there was no one there. A table moved. This was poltergeist activity as the table was heavy. We took photographs and then things moved. We were in the area of the house where people call the police, as they see people inside.

The Tudor House Museum.

UK PRS does not investigate the history of a property until after they have visited it and studied it, so there is no chance of bias. The investigators also take along mediums to the properties they visit

Keivan White is a medium who came along to the Tudor House Museum. He was able to give names of people he was in contact with there, who we later researched. Southampton City Council gave full access to their archive. Their staff were fascinated and came along every day.

The Medieval Merchants House

Fifty-eight French Street holds a special place in the hearts of locals. It stands out because it is the only medieval house still standing in what is now an area covered in flats and commercial buildings.

It is one of the earliest surviving houses in England, dating from the end of the thirteenth century, and was a place of residence as well as commercial premises. John Fortin, a wine merchant, built it for his family. It survived damage at the hands of the French in 1338 and the Germans during the Second World War.

Over time it has been divided into tenement flats, refurbished back into one house and used as Mrs Collins's Lodging House for Theatricals. It was called the Bull's Head Inn in the nineteenth century, when an unseen spirit blew out cellar candles unexpectedly.

The Medieval Merchants House.

Ian Fox tells the tale of Sarah Jane Allen, who married the owner's son and lived at the house for a year in 1900. She told her granddaughter that when she woke up in the mornings there was often a woman's ghost standing at the end of the bed, wearing a dirty white or grey dress. She vanished when Mrs Allen moved to rouse her husband.

The house became seedier and was used as a brothel for a time. During the Second World War a prostitute is said to have killed a sailor at the house when he disputed the cost of her services.

One medium who investigated the property was certain that the spirit of someone who had committed suicide in a room upstairs still resides there. The man had been suffering from a 'social disease'.

A local theatrical group used the property as their headquarters for more than twenty years and there were numerous sightings and strange occurrences reported during this time. Footsteps were heard on the wooden staircase, a spectral female shape would be seen in an upstairs room and this would drift through the wall at a point where there was a bricked-up doorway, the heavy doors at the front of the house would slam shut by themselves and people would feel themselves pushed when up on the open landing.

At a séance held there, a woman called Ruth Dill made contact. She is said to have told the medium that in life she had liked to steal jewellery and had killed a sailor for his treasure, which she had then thrown down a well. Despite searching, the truth of this statement is still in doubt.

The property is now a tourist attraction owned by English Heritage. During its refurbishment, workers reported lights in the huge cellar inexplicably dimming or going out and, at four one afternoon, an unearthly chill crept across the house.

The Bargate

The 800-year-old Bargate was originally the main gateway into the medieval city of Southampton. It has had an interesting history, being the Guildhall in the eighteenth century, a fire station in the early twentieth century and the police HQ during the Second World War. It is now known as the Bargate Monument Gallery, after a major refurbishment, which saw it reopen to the public as an art gallery in 2006.

'The Bargate would be leased out for art exhibitions and such like, and weird things would happen,' says paranormal investigator, Andrew House. 'Bell ringing and things moving – was it drunks or was something going on? An *Echo* reporter left, scared, after a huge, unexplained bang upstairs, and footsteps were heard during our investigation. The Bargate, though, is not as active as the Tudor House.'

Below: *The Bargate has a long history.*

COUNTY BOROUGH OF SOUTHAMPTON

BARGATE
AND
GUILDHALL

DURING THE 12TH. CENTURY THIS
NORTHERN GATEWAY TO THE
MEDIEVAL TOWN WAS A SINGLE
ROUND ARCHWAY.
IN THE 13TH. CENTURY TWO ROUND
TOWERS WERE ADDED AND EARLY
IN THE 15TH. CENTURY THE NORTH
FRONT WAS EXTENDED
· · ·
THE GUILDHALL NOW A MUSEUM
WAS FORMERLY THE TOWN'S
ADMINISTRATIVE CENTRE
AND USED FOR PUBLIC FUNCTIONS
AND FOR PERFORMANCES BY
COMPANIES OF STROLLING PLAYERS

Above: *The Bargate today – many locals do not realise they are walking past a haunted building!*

Snippets Around The City

J.P. Chilcott-Monk gives several passing references to ghostly activities in and around Southampton (*Ghosts of South Hampshire and Beyond*, Part One).

In St Denys there was a sighting of a 'curious, misty display at night'. The report was of a 'humanesque amoeba of fluffy mist', which floated around gardens in the area.

Older Portswood residents may remember the Tapper furniture shop. When it first opened, a passing shopper collapsed outside and was taken inside the store, to rest on a sofa in the window. Sadly, she died there and forever afterwards many people entering the store reported 'strange and weird sensations' as they walked through the door.

A sobbing, soaking wet, young girl is sometimes seen on Northam Bridge. Police picked her up on one occasion. They asked her for her address and put her in their patrol car to drive her home. When they pulled up in Thornhill, or, in some reports, near the bridge, she had vanished from the car. When the police officers knocked on the door of the address they had been given, they were told that the girl had died some months earlier.

The Hexham Heads

Wendy Boase tells the strange and disturbing tale of the 1971-72 events involving carved stone heads in Southampton. The website Mysterious Britain goes into some detail about the same story. Dr Anne Ross, the celebrated author of such works as *Pagan Celtic Britain* (1967), and a noted Celtic scholar, was at the centre of a drama, which some might describe as unnerving.

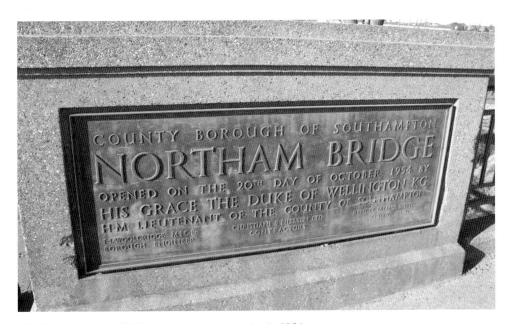

The plaque on Northam Bridge, commemorating its opening in 1954.

The young sons of the Robson family dug up the heads in their garden in Hexham, near Hadrian's Wall. The heads, each about the size of an orange, became known as the Hexham Heads and two were sent to Dr Ross's home for her to study. Two days after receiving them, she was woken up in the early hours of the morning, as she was cold and felt frightened. She followed a dark, half-man, half-beast, shadowy figure from her bathroom to the bottom of her staircase. This figure she later described on the Mysterious Britain website, as, 'About 6ft high, slightly stooping, and it was black, against the white door, and it was half animal and half man. The upper part was a wolf, and the lower part was human and it was covered with a kind of black, very dark fur.' Terrified, she then returned to the bedroom to wake her husband, archaeologist, Richard Feacham. Although they searched the house, they could find no trace of the figure she had seen.

The couple's teenage daughter, Berenice, returned to an empty house after school a short time later and was startled to see a large, dark figure on the stairs. This darted away towards the girl's room and, although as terrified as her mother had been, she felt she should follow him. At the doorway to the bedroom, the figure disappeared, leaving the girl very shocked. Once again, a search of the house proved fruitless.

Dr Ross continued to feel the presence of something in the house, and often heard the sound of padded feet near the stairs. The study door would fling itself open suddenly, and the strange figure was again glimpsed on the stairs.

Over a year later, when the heads were no longer in the house, Dr Ross learnt that the same shadowy, half-man, half-beast figure had appeared to Ellen Dodd and her daughter, whose home was next door to the Robsons' garden. The woman was very disturbed by the incident, but a thorough search did not reveal any trace of the figure.

Dr Ross felt that the heads contained some kind of evil influence and were used as shrine guards. Thus, when they were disturbed, a malevolent spirit was released. Locally in Hexham, a link between the shadowy figure and the legendary Wolf of Allendale, which caused havoc amongst livestock in 1904, is spoken of.

The Hexham Heads were exhibited in the British Museum for some time, before being taken off public display.

The Brunswick Place Ghost

Christine Bagg tells the tale of when she was a temp at the solicitors, Ewing, Hickman & Clark in Brunswick Place in Southampton's city centre.

Tales of the ghost haunting these offices go back many years. Beloved Southampton historian, Elsie Sandell, recounted the tale of ghostly footsteps being heard in offices here in her book, *Southampton Cavalcade* in the 1950s. What is generally not known is that these footsteps have not gone away!

Christine takes up the tale:

My encounter with the supernatural occurred in 2000, on my first day at work as a temporary legal secretary at Ewing, Hickman & Clark, as the firm was then known. Their premises were a three-storey Georgian House in Brunswick Place, Southampton, opposite the park.

James Archibald Ewing founded the firm in 1900. Humphrey Hickman joined the firm in 1925 with Harvey Clark joining just after the Second World War. I was working on the top floor, which consisted of three offices for secretaries, and a cloakroom.

At lunchtime I went to the cloakroom, and while I was washing my hands I heard footsteps coming up the stairs and into the office where I worked. I quickly dried my hands on the towel and stepped across the landing into the room. To my surprise it was completely empty. I had the feeling someone was looking for me so I went into the other two offices, but they were also empty. All the girls had gone to lunch and there was no one there. Thinking it strange but not feeling particularly disturbed, I collected my handbag and went out.

Later that afternoon I mentioned what I had heard. I was told that old Mr Ewing used to live on the third floor, over the firm. When he died, in his flat, the floor was converted into secretarial space. The room I worked in had been Mr Ewings' personal quarters, where he spent a lot of time. I was told that he was often heard walking around the top floor but no one had ever seen him. The other girls didn't seem at all worried about the presence of a ghost at work and the atmosphere there was always happy. I returned to work at Ewing, Hickman & Clark many times over the years, on the top floor, but I never heard those footsteps again.

Gillian Clark, Harvey Clark's daughter, who is a partner in the firm now known as Footner & Ewing, says of James Ewing: 'My father used to say what a gentle and charming man he was, so I am sure if he does visit occasionally, it is very benevolently.'

This gentle story is another to add to Southampton's rich store of ghostly tales.

The Station Pub, Bitterne

The relative newcomer in the pub world, Gusto Inns, runs The Station pub, on Bullar Road, near the railway station in Bitterne, which gives it its name. The sign outside proudly states that it dates from about 1880 and it has been extended and enlarged

The Station public house, Bitterne.

over the years to its present imposing size on the substantial corner plot, overlooking the busy junction at the bottom of Lances Hill.

Adele Stevens has worked at The Station for four and a half years. Now the manager, she has experienced, or heard of, some of the supernatural activity the staff live with on a daily basis. She says:

We have a couple of ghosts! There is a male and a female and one we are not sure about.

There is a lady in the ladies' bathroom. Nothing has ever happened to me in there but there have been reports of people getting tapped on the shoulder, making them jump, and things like that. It is the spirit of a lady who used to drink in here, we think. She was one of our regulars many years ago and where she used to sit at the end of the bar is where the ladies' toilets are now. Then, before the extension was built, the end of the bar turned around the corner, where the toilets are now, and that is where she is.

The remodelled bar, with the entrance to the ladies' restroom in the background. Originally the bar curved around, through the area that is now the ladies' room.

The Station pub's cellar – note the open door in the background.

This lady is not the only spirit in residence at The Station. The cellar seems to hold a certain fascination.

Adele takes up the story:

The cellar, we call it the Ghost Room, is basically just a boiler room. If you ever shut the door then it (the spirit) goes a bit crazy and throws everything around. It is our junk room, we have our Christmas decorations and bits like that there, and when we have new staff come in we tell them never to shut the door because if you go down there again then everything will be everywhere.

A few months ago I went down there to put the delivery away, on a Thursday. The bottles just get left at the bottom of the drop hatch. Some go in a cold drum and some stay in crates. A few hours later I went down there to change a barrel and to finish putting all the crates away on a stack of shelves we put them on. There was a crate of Red Bull upside down in the middle of the floor and an hour before I had put that crate on the shelf. I thought, someone is having a laugh, and so I put it back, went upstairs, came back down a couple of hours later and it was sitting in the middle of the floor, upside down again. I thought, well, no one else has been down here. I know no one else had been down there. I just told them to stop messing around and after that it was fine.

In the cellar I reckon it's a little boy because he likes playing around with the Christmas decorations or things like that. But, we have never proved anything.

It is not just the ladies' bathroom and the cellar, which are haunted. The kitchen too has had its fair share of supernatural activity. Adele says:

You would think it would be in the middle of the night when no one's here but the main things happen in the daytime. There was another incident a couple of years ago. There was

Above: *The kitchen at The Station, Bitterne.*

Left: *The Ghost Room.*

27

the chef, Gary, and the ex-landlady, Kerry, and I, who were in the kitchen and chatting about Mother's Day or something, and we were just standing there. I stood this side, facing Kerry and Gary who were the other side of the kitchen. We have a stack of kitchen shelves, which had plates on them at the time, and, all of a sudden, the top lot of plates just flew off and dropped to the floor. That freaked me out. I walked out then. It wasn't as if the wind just blew them or something, they went out a couple of feet from the shelving, stayed in the air for a second and then dropped.

The current dry store, which used to be part of the men's bathroom before the extensive renovations, is another place where staff have experienced unexplained happenings. Adele explains:

One of the bar staff went in to speak to Gary, the chef. She walked in and could hear whistling and thought oh, he's out the back in the dry store. She walked on through and she shouted, and the whistling stopped. She went out the back and no one was there. She came out to the bar area, told myself and Gary, who had missed her by coming out to talk to me, and then walked out the door. She was a bit freaked out but she was all right after, in a couple of days. She carried on and it only happened the once.

Adele wonders if this male whistler is the same spirit who appeared on the CCTV monitors many times:

I think he walks from the pool table to the kitchen. When we used to have a monitor, for the CCTV, we had a camera up to monitor the premises. It's a big pub, and late at night on

The pool table at The Station. The ghost likes to stand under the left-hand lamp at the far end of the room.

the monitor, sometimes you would be able to see a figure standing in the corner, and, when you went down there and walked into the left corner, it would instantly go cold. The lights were reflected from outside and if you pulled the blinds and had a look it was still there, a kind of an outline of a figure standing in the corner.

Who was this tall spirit, who stood up against the wall, almost to the height of the lampshades? Adele is unable to say.

The Station has never been the subject of a formal paranormal investigation. This is because as Adele says:

I believe in the paranormal but I do not want to mess around with it, if you know what I mean. I leave them alone and they leave me alone. I am here on my own quite early in the morning some times and it is just like... nah!

She shakes her head with a smile.

We have never lost any staff. If something happens to them they get a bit freaked out and they won't go in the cellar for a week. That is the main place where things happen really, the cellar. We warn them when they come. On the first day we tell them The Station is haunted. If they shut the door the spirits will play around. If you leave them alone, they leave you alone and that is the way it's always been really. They get a bit freaked out though.

The Station was a John Barras pub and there is a portrait of John Barras Jnr on the wall, celebrating the opening of the John Barras & Co. brewing business in 1770. This was started by John Barras Snr and his partner, William Johnstone. On the death of his father, in 1811, John Barras Jnr set in motion the expansion that eventually saw the company own a string of public houses.

The Brewery was merged several times and today the name remains as one of the reminders of the founding fathers of the brewing industry.

Bitterne Manor

Bitterne Manor is famous for its notorious bend in the dual carriageway, which has caused many an unwary, fast-driving motorist to come to grief when trying to negotiate it. The 30mph speed limit may have slowed drivers, but reported sightings of ghostly Roman legionnaires in the area have certainly not helped the unsuspecting motorists.

The Roman Clausentum, or Roman station, which is believed to have been a supply and storage depot in the area, was the home to Roman legions up to about AD 410, shortly after Roman rule in Britain ended. Single or massed groups of ghostly figures are sometimes seen on the bend as they march across, ignoring the traffic bearing down upon them. According to Ian Fox, reports of sightings were particularly numerous in the early 1950s, when the new Northam Bridge was being

The suburb of Bitterne Manor, where Roman legionnaires wander.

built over the River Itchen. Perhaps they did not like their peace being disturbed? Sightings have been reported since and Fox details the experience of a now-retired bank manager, who wished to remain anonymous, as he was afraid of ridicule.

The incident took place in October 1981, as the bank manager was driving home from a long day at the city centre bank branch where he worked. As he drove around the bend at Bitterne Manor, he saw a figure move out from the left-hand side and start to cross the road without regard to the oncoming cars. The bank manager thought at first that it was someone being careless but then realised that he could only see the man from the knees upwards. It was as if he was walking on ground that was lower than the road is now. The figure was not clear but he had the distinct impression of it being a Roman soldier, wearing what he described as a 'short, swishing tunic and something on his head, perhaps a helmet.' The bank manager braked sharply and missed the figure, which 'dissolved' as he reached the centre of the dual carriageway. Considerably shaken, he went home and told only his wife and, later, his deputy at the bank. He was reassured by the fact that his deputy had heard similar stories before.

Shadows in Freemantle

Chris Mould often sees shadows at his Freemantle home. 'You see someone in your peripheral vision and when you look round, nobody is there,' he says, clearly perplexed.

His home is also subject to strange smells. 'At home, in our bedroom, now and again you get a really strong cigarette smell. We don't smoke! Our next-door neighbours don't smoke either, so if the windows are open, it is not wafting in from there.'

Perhaps the spirit, whose shadow Chris sometimes catches sight of, was fond of a sly puff now and again!

A Poltergeist in Freemantle

You have to feel sorry for Barry Kinceh. For years, he and his partner, Anne, have been plagued by a booze-loving poltergeist at their home in Norman Road, Freemantle.

'I have a poltergeist in my house!' He explains:

All sorts of ridiculous things happen – things disappear. They vanish off the face of the earth: cutlery, glasses, cans of beer and all sorts of things.

I was in the kitchen one evening and I put my can of beer on the corner of the worktop. The bathroom is about 3ft away. I walked through the door to the bathroom and I was in there for just three minutes. I came out, went to the can but that beer had gone. I went in to Anne and said, "Have you nicked my beer? " "I haven't moved from the telly," she replied. It was not very funny at the time. I ended up blaming my partner for something she didn't do!

Another time, on the anniversary of our friend's death, I poured her favourite tipple, vodka and orange, and put it on the side for her. That disappeared, along with the glass as well; everything disappeared! Cutlery goes left, right and centre, too. You put teaspoons out and they go. It is not like they have been lost or mislaid, they vanish. Occasionally, they turn up again – about a year later.

Barry Kinceh outside his house in Freemantle, which he shares with his partner Anne and a booze-loving poltergeist!

Roger Green

Sometimes it seems that strange happenings will follow someone throughout their life. Woolston resident, Roger Green, seems to be one such person.

As a child, Roger lived in Selborne Road, on the Harefield Estate, just off the West End Road. When he was fourteen, he and his friends would go off into the surrounding countryside; the Townhill Park estate had not then been built and there was farmland all around the area:

> We used to come up the hill from Selborne Road. There was a steep bank, it might be people's back gardens now, but we used to go in there and walk down through and you could go right the way across to Hatch Farm. There were not many trees but there were hedgerows. There were odd trees in the fields. It was just there, behind the nunnery, that I would hear someone playing the bagpipes – always in the same field and always on the other side of the bushes. When we used to dive around there, there was nobody there.

Roger's favourite fishing spot is just along from the old Supermarine Spitfire site in Woolston:

> I go fishing, down on the end of the jetty in the middle of the river in Woolston – I have the keys to the gate there. My son and I fish until three or four in the morning, my son at one end of the point and me at the other. One night an aeroplane went over. It was a clear night and I was looking for it and I thought, there's no plane. There was just no plane and it was two o'clock in the morning. I thought when I first looked up, No! That's late going in to the airport, but there was nothing there, and you would definitely see it as you would see the lights on it. It sounded like a small plane but there was nothing there at all.

From unexplained sounds to a different phenomenon, Roger takes up the story again:

> After my first wife, Shirley, died, the bottom of the bed went up and down, while I was in it. It was as if someone was sitting on it, or putting their hands on it and pressing the mattress up and down. It went on for quite a long time. It didn't bother me but it was strange.
>
> Shirley died at Christmas time. Three weeks before Christmas, she asked me to put up the Christmas tree, so I rushed and did it. I put the tree up and decorated it. We had a fairy that used to sit up on the top. It was an old fairy. It was odd that year as it kept tipping over and Shirley said, "That fairy, can you put it up straight? It keeps looking at me." Every time I righted it, it just kept tipping over again, in exactly the same position.'

Was this significant? Roger thinks so, particularly as the nocturnal mattress bouncing kept up for some time after his wife's death.

However, the strangest story comes from Roger's home in John's Road, Woolston, which he shares with his second wife, Julie:

When I first met Julie, twenty years ago, I stood in the kitchen leaning against the kitchen worktop, and I felt something by my leg, rubbing it. I looked down and just as I looked down, a cat went across the room and straight through the wall opposite. I just looked at it and thought, No! I told Julie and she said that it had been seen before. It was a mottled colour and I only saw it the once.

The wall now goes into next door. It was formerly a coalhouse at the back of the property. The cat might have been here before the house was built. I don't know.

It is up to the reader to decide on the merits of this case, but it seems strange that so many unexplained events happen to one particular person.

Meanwhile, Julie says of her experience of ghostly phenomena in the house:

Up until the one house was partitioned to make it into two houses you could walk into the back bedroom. I took the camera up there one day and just went 'click'. There were orbs, loads of them, in the picture. I took one the next day and there were two. I thought, well, there might be something in this.

Tatwin Crescent

'Strange goings-on' is the way Ian Fox describes the events that went on at Tatwin Crescent in Thornhill in the early 1970s.

The Southampton public libraries archive service has preserved the original *Echo* report by Keith Hamilton, 'Unwelcome visitors whose call brings terror'. It makes fascinating reading, bringing a chill to the spine of even the most sceptical of readers.

Life at the council flats at the time is described as a 'living nightmare'. The residents, many of whom were young mothers, were being plagued by 'ghostly figures whispering and moaning; taps coming on by themselves in the middle of the night; furniture and clothes mysteriously thrown about' and much else.

Tatwin Crescent, the scene of poltergeist activity in the 1970s.

The ghostly goings-on always happened in the winter months and one resident is quoted as saying that she 'dreads' them and, 'It is at this time of the year when all these horrible things happen.'

She was startled by the figure of a man appearing in her hallway, and her neighbour was very upset by hearing and seeing a man letting himself in through her front door and then walking towards the living room where she was sitting, before vanishing just before the sitting room door. When she investigated the front door, it was still locked, exactly as she had left it. She thought she had a poltergeist in her flat, a conviction that was reinforced by the appearance of the same man by her bedside a little while later and by the fact that her stove in the kitchen started moving by itself, rocking about so violently that plates sitting on the top rattled.

The reports of strange happenings at the flats were so numerous that the flats were exorcised. This, however, proved fruitless as unexplained events continued after the service.

One couple was so upset by the atmosphere in their home, and by fact that the piano kept playing by itself and frightening their babysitter, that they moved out, and insisted on smashing the piano up instead of taking it with them to their new Shirley home.

Another resident saw a figure on her balcony, which kept calling her name softly. She also claimed to hear moaning and heavy breathing behind her as she moved about the flat, and to have found ornaments in her living room scattered on the floor in the mornings.

The stories about Tatwin Crescent seemed to go on and on. Another resident reported that her taps kept being turned on at night. She is quoted as saying, 'They were turned full on and so far round I could not turn them off. It was as if someone was stopping me.' She also recounted the time that she and her husband were watching television and realised that a man was pushing his face up against the glass door to the living room. Her husband jumped up to investigate, but the face disappeared and there was no one there. Once again, the front door was locked. When her husband was killed in a car accident near Basingstoke in 1973, the new widow was startled to see the doors of the wardrobe in their bedroom opening of their own accord just days later and one of her husband's suits came flying out and landed neatly on the bed. Not surprisingly, Mrs Allen wanted to move out of the flat. 'These flats have become a living nightmare,' she said at the time.

Tatwin Crescent had, apparently, been built on the grounds of an old house. At the end of the nineteenth century, during a particularly bad winter, people sleeping rough there had perished. Was it the spirits of these unfortunates, who were now unsettling the residents of the flats? We shall probably never know.

The Haunting in Colebrook Avenue, Upper Shirley

Sue Wardall freely admits she was sceptical about ghosts. That is, until she and her family moved into No. 13 Colebrook Avenue in Shirley. This is because, for the first six months they lived there, the nights were punctuated by strange events that they have found no explanation for.

Sue's husband and son found themselves getting up and turning off the family's electronic toothbrushes, which had all come on simultaneously at two o'clock in the morning. They were not plugged into the mains to re-charge, and they could find no reason for them all, four of them, to start whirring away at the same instant.

Just after eleven one evening Sue was in the house by herself, upstairs. She takes up the story:

> I was in my bedroom and my son's bedroom backs on to mine. His music player came on loudly. I didn't hear him come in, but, assuming he was home, I called out to say turn it off. Then I opened his door gently. My son wasn't there but his music was playing away. It wasn't very nice to go into his room – it was in darkness and the music was loud.

Sue clearly does not enjoy looking back on this incident.

Other occurrences in the house included a neatly stacked pile of CDs falling to the floor for no apparent reason. However, the event that upset the household the most was the crash Sue, her husband and son heard late one night. Sue says:

> One night I was reading. It was at about the same time as the music went on in my son's bedroom. I was lying in bed and it was below me, in the dining room; the heaviest thing breaking. I thought, oh, my god; somebody's dropped the laptop! I mean, it was a real crash and it was in the house. I got up and thought that whatever has been dropped is broken and it's expensive. I came downstairs and my son and my husband were in the store cupboard.

The family thought that the noise had come from there but Sue, upstairs, thought it had come from within the house itself, not the cupboard. 'When I saw them looking, they said, "What was that?" and I said, "I'm coming down to ask you the same question." It was horrendously loud. The crash was frightening because it was so loud.'

So upset were the family – who had managed to keep the strange events from their daughter, who would have been very upset by them – that when a friend suggested that they might have a spirit in the house and advised them to stand up to it, Sue took the advice seriously:

> Someone told me to say, 'Go home, whatever you are, wherever you are, leave us alone.' I felt a bit of a prat but I did it and that was it. Everything just stopped. Nothing has happened since. I feel though that it's not my home now. If ever I am in a position to leave it, I will.

The Old Farmhouse

Barrie Short, the landlord of the Grade II listed Old Farmhouse public house in Mount Pleasant Road, is a bit sceptical about ghosts. 'I don't believe!' he firmly declares from his niche at one side of the long bar in Southampton's oldest pub.

The Old Farmhouse was once just that, a farmhouse standing amidst meadows alongside the River Itchen. It is rumoured that Oliver Cromwell once stayed there and there are old smugglers' tunnels running from the building's fireplace to two points outside. Pictures of the building at various stages through its long history adorn the walls of the olde-worlde, low-ceilinged, wood beamed building that oozes charm and a sense of peace that comes with great age. One, a line drawing dated 1821 by an unknown hand, graphically illustrates the changes that both the building and the surrounding area have undergone since the farmhouse was built in 1611.

The farmhouse became a public house in 1843. Today it is a thriving concern under the friendly eyes of Barrie and his wife, Jo, and stands near the busy main railway line between London and Weymouth. The picturesque meadows have long disappeared.

'Mind you,' says Barrie, obviously thinking better of what he has just so fervently declared, 'there have been a few weird things happen here, now I come to think of it.' He goes on:

The Old Farmhouse. (Photograph courtesy of Barrie and Jo Short)

We understand that there was an Irish family who used to live here when the place was still a farmhouse. The daughter of the family got pregnant out of wedlock and disappeared soon afterwards. A skull was found in the cellar and it used to sit out on the shelf behind the bar but is now no longer there. I have been here for six years and it has not been there in my time.

I try not to go into the loft if I can help it. [At this point Barrie shivers visibly.] I know that whenever I go up there something weird will happen soon afterwards. The jukebox will play strange music for the next couple of days or the television will continually change channels, despite our not having touched the remote control. There is nothing you can put your finger on – nothing is broken or wrong – but for a couple of days after I go to the loft odd things happen and then things are right as rain again.

The room now housing the pool table was the original kitchen to the farmhouse and still has the ovens and range along one wall, perfectly preserved. It would have been this room that was the heart of the house. Could it be that it was here that the family met to discuss what to do with the errant daughter and her unwanted unborn baby? What did happen to her, and was it her skull that was found in the cellar? Is her spirit still in the house, perhaps abiding quietly in the loft? Is she showing her displeasure at being disturbed when Barrie has to go up into the loft, by making her presence felt? We will probably never know the truth, but one thing is for sure, Barrie is not so adamant in his disbelief of the spirit world as he once was.

Leighton Road, Sholing

Things that go bump in the night have long fascinated Kelly Leigh and her brother, Lee Davies. The ghost that haunted their grandparents' home frightened them and they have never forgotten. They take it in turns to tell the tale. Lee says:

Leighton Road, Sholing.

Many years ago, when we were children we were at Dad's parents' place down in Leighton Road, Sholing. It started with a story about the neighbour who did not live in the house; he lived in the shed. I can't remember why, but he lived there and died there. Even though he had family in his house, he stayed in the shed. That is what I remember. When he died, his spirit appeared in the house opposite, which was our grandparents' home. They ended up getting an exorcism done. Our dad told us the story. We just thought, yeah, he's trying to frighten us – until he was fixing the back door one day. My mum was in the back of the house with my nan, Kelly was making the tea and I said, 'I'll go and get the cups, where are they?' 'On the shelf,' I was told.

Kelly takes up the tale: 'The crockery was on a massive, old-fashioned dresser. The set was white with blue painted patterns on it. Nan had all the teacups and saucers set out.'

'I went to go grab them,' says Lee, 'and every single one of them got up and shook. They rattled against each other. The saucers rattled against the wood, the cups against the saucers, everything on three or four shelves. I ran, Kelly ran, even the dog ran!'

'We were talking about the spirit at the time,' says Kelly. 'Nan had a very big, old-fashioned, heavy, wooden door with the old turn handles. The door kept opening into the kitchen and we thought it was our mum. But she was with our nan at the time. Then, as Lee went to pick up the cups, everything just lifted and shook.'

'We did not like going upstairs to the toilet in that house,' Lee remembers. 'Halfway up the stairs it went cold, just like that. Even just looking up the corridor towards the stairs freaked you out. None of us would go to the toilet on our own – Kelly came with me.'

'That's right,' says Kelly. 'We never went on our own, ever. Even waiting outside the bathroom for the other one, whether the light was on or off you did not like it, it was very eerie. I would not go back into the house now, not even at my age.'

The house is currently empty.

These events took place when Kelly was nine and Lee six, but their legacy has remained with them in the form of a shudder when they think of their grandparents' home and a paradoxical desire to visit haunted properties. They joined several other enthusiasts in the investigation made by the Southampton-based company, Haunted Southampton, at The Red Lion pub in Southampton's High Street.

Romill Close, West End

Rob Butler has been fascinated by the paranormal for as long as he can remember. 'I have always been interested,' he says. 'I don't know why but since I was a child I have been interested in creepy movies and the paranormal. I borrowed books from the library on ghosts and spirits as a teenager. Not that I witnessed anything as a child, but I have always been curious about things like that.'

This curiosity led to Rob applying to join Southern Paranormal UK, an investigation group that began in 2005, started by Poole-based investigator, Julie Harwood.

'I was forty last year and I said to my partner, 'For my fortieth what I would like to do is join a team, because we had occurrences at Romill.'

The 'Romill' Rob is referring to is Romill Close, in West End. For several years Rob, his partner Fran and their two daughters, lived at No. 2, a semi-detached cottage, adjoining their landlord's property.

'My partner, Fran, was living there with her daughter Aleasha before I moved in,' Rob explains.

Nearly six years ago I moved in. It was a nice little cottage; homely. I remember the very first day I moved in with all my boxes. I was taking them up into the bedroom and unpacking them one by one. I came back downstairs and Aleasha was in the dining room with Fran. As I came downstairs, and stepped off the last step, there was an almighty crash behind me. We all looked and there was a box on the stairs. I had my back to the stairs and couldn't see what had gone on. Fran had to tell Aleasha, who was only six at the time, that I must have dropped it behind me. She went off quite happily, but Fran then told me how she saw the box actually flying through the air. Normally when a box falls it would bounce downstairs. This one hit the wall with such force it was like it was thrown. We thought nothing of it, as you do. You explain it away.

Then, a couple of weeks later, we heard tapping noises. We thought, what was that? We would also smell bread baking. We knew the landlord's house was directly next-door, as we were semi-detached. We would put our heads out the door but we couldn't smell it outside. We could only smell it in one room in the house, our lounge.

We then started seeing shadows – corner of the eye things. Fran would say, 'Did you see that?' These shadows looked like someone had just walked past the front door, or they would

Pretty Romill Close. No. 2 is very active!

be a shadow on the wall. We would go out and I would walk up the driveway to see if I could recreate the shadows. We are both like that, we try to debunk things before we start thinking that something wasn't right.

We would be lying in bed and we would hear scratching. One night, we had seen quite a few shadows in the dining room on the walls, we heard someone tapping their fingers on the bedside table and the lamp started rocking. Fran was sleeping that side. We had been in bed about half an hour and were just at that drop off stage. All of a sudden Fran said, 'It's the lamp!' It stopped rocking and then we heard tap, tap, tap on the bedside cabinet. I said to Fran, 'You have to turn the light on!' We then sat there for half an hour trying to see if we could rock the lamp. Could it have been a breeze? It would not move, even with us rocking the bedside table. We knew then, in our own minds. The fact that we both heard it validates it. It was two people witnessing it, even though it was dark. I thought something is not right here; something is going on in this house.

The tapping became such a common event that Rob and Fran encouraged it:

Sometimes we would call out, is there anyone there? Can you tap if there is anyone there? Can you tap twice? We would hear tap, tap. It would freak us out! But, at the end of the day, wow! We always got replies, all the time. Once we were in bed I would call out, 'Is there anyone there?' We would not see it but it felt like the bedroom door was being shaken. You could hear it. Again, it was a case of light on quick, nothing there. The moment the light went off, the tapping started again. We did the obvious and checked for rats in the house or birds in the loft but there was nothing at all. It was a sound cottage, even though it was old.

We started to look into the history of the place. It was built on wet pastures. No. 1 Romill Close used to be called Romill House. The earliest plans we found went back to 1570. On this plan, right in the area where numbers one and two are now, is the cottage.

Thus, it would seem that the current properties were once one building and were partitioned off into two semi-detached houses, at some time in the past. Rob continued:

The worst times for us were in 2008 and 2009. We had a lot of things being moved then. It was out of sight movement; only once did we see something move in front of us. A lot of the time, we would go out of the room, come back and something would be moved. We have a red dice, which I use in my investigations. We were in the lounge one night and we heard tap, tap, roll. Then it stopped. We thought, what is that? I wondered if it was the dice that we had left out in the conservatory and so we went out there. All the windows were shut. We put the dice back where it had been and went to the front room. Five minutes later, we heard, tap, tap, tap, roll on the floor again. There was no one in there, no breeze, nothing. Fran said it was coming up with different numbers and wondered if someone was trying to tell us a date? The amount of time the dice rolled, there is no date possible! We wondered all different things. Was it someone trying to get in touch with us? Was it a child? Was it an adult? What could it be, we wondered?

This strange photograph of the interior of No. 2, Romill Close, was taken by Rob Butler, who cannot explain the distortion. (Photograph courtesy of Rob Butler)

We went online and tried Ancestry.com, where you can find out the old deeds of the areas of where you live. That area used to be the area of South Stoneham. Stoneham church is just behind the cottage. We managed to research the house back to 1820, when a family called the Jellymans' used to live there. The father worked in a paper mill, the mother was a laundry mistress, doing washing for people, and they had five children. One of the youngest died in the house of an unknown illness, when they were eleven. I think the father's name was Charles Jellyman. We were interested in the child who died of the unknown illness.

I will always remember one night, two years ago. I have been an insomniac for years, waking up at certain times in the night and not being able to go back to sleep. One night I woke up and I went downstairs. I am a smoker, so I thought I would go to the conservatory and have a cigarette. I put the dining room light on. We had a lounge, dining room, kitchen, and conservatory and we smoked out the back. All of a sudden, I felt funny. I felt really sick and headachy. I thought it was that I had just woken from a deep sleep and put it down to that. Then, as I looked round, in the doorway of the dining room into the front room, was a white mist. It was a white fog. In the centre of this fog was the outline of a boy, a young boy. He was looking at me and he had his arms out, palms up. It was there but like looking through a sheet of tracing paper. You could still see things behind but they were very blurred. I tell you, that is the one time that I have seen a full body apparition, and I have to be honest, I said a few choice words! I blinked and he was gone. By that time, I was sweating and I was crying. I quickly shut the conservatory door, ran upstairs and woke my partner up. I was in a state of fright; she had to get out of bed. I was leaning on the door saying, 'I can't believe what I have just seen.' 'What have you seen,' she said. 'What was it?' I told her and I was hyperventilating – I was in a right state.

The boy had long hair, and reminded Rob of pictures he had seen of children in about the eighteenth century. The clothing was indistinct and so Rob could not be certain what the apparition was wearing. Rob continued:

> It was definitely a young child's form with his palms out, I don't know why he appeared or what he was doing – perhaps he was shrugging his shoulders – but that is what I saw. I can't explain the mist. It was there and then it wasn't.
>
> I remember one night, we were all sitting in the dining room and we heard this almighty bang on the top of our landing. We then heard drop, drop, drop, drop and Fran said that it sounded like the dice. I remember we had it on the top of the unit in our bedroom. We used to say to the spirits, 'If you want to play with it, there it is.' There was a definite thud as it hit the wall, then it rattled down the stairs.
>
> We had our friends around, Carl and Kerry, two days later. They like stories about the paranormal, so we were describing to them what had happened with the dice. I said, 'This is what happened,' and threw it at the bottom stair. It then rolled right under the other side of the dining table. When we looked on the floor for it, the dice had gone. We had looked away for an instant, chatting. I said to Carl, 'Where is the dice?' 'What do you mean?' he replied. It was then spotted by my partner's foot, 10ft from the table. How had it got there without us knowing about it or seeing it? I said to Carl, 'Do you realise that if I had looked back half a second ago I would have seen it in the air levitating!' He said, 'If I had seen it, I would have been out of here!'

It was after these experiences that Rob joined Southern Paranormal UK:

> My first contact when we had these experiences was with Maria Street, one of the Senior Coordinators of Southern Paranormal. I rang her, she gave me a bit of advice about the experiences we were having and then I applied to join the team. They accepted me as a member and I have not looked back. I have been on thirty or forty investigations.

Testwood House, near Totton

The property was first known as Little Testwood and its owner at that time was Sir Richard Dayrell, who farmed large estates and entertained on a grand scale in fifteenth-century Hampshire.

In its time this house was a hunting lodge frequented by royalty, a private house, a club and the offices of a firm of sherry shippers. There are different versions of the tale, which revolves around the cook, the victim of murder most foul, who was killed at the house and her body dragged to Cook's Lane on the far side of the Salisbury Road. Opinions vary as to the identity of the killer. Some say he was the coachman, some a groom and others, a butler.

Another version of the story suggest a love triangle, with the coachman killing the butler over a woman.

Peter Underwood, in *The A-Z of British Ghosts*, Ian Fox in *The Haunted Places of Hampshire* and Wendy Boase, in her excellent, *The Folklore of Hampshire and the Isle of Wight*, all mention Testwood as being haunted.

According to Ian Fox, an early ghost hunter, Stephen Darby, kept a record of Hampshire hauntings at the turn of the twentieth century. He mentioned ghostly figures, including that of a dog on the drive, and also that the sounds of a coach and horses were often heard approaching the house.

All three writers cite the experiences of the caretaker who was employed by Williams & Humbert, the sherry importers at Testwood. It was he who was the first to hear ghostly footsteps, which sounded as if they were on bare boards when the floors were then covered in thick carpeting. The footsteps were said to come from one particular corridor, which, so the story goes, dogs refused to walk down. Williams & Humbert took over the premises in 1958.

In 1961, the caretaker's teenage son and daughter saw a man trying to enter the house, who vanished when they challenged him.

The Willams & Humbert chef, working late one evening, was startled to see a man standing silently beside him in the kitchen. The man vanished almost as soon as the chef became aware of his presence. Later, the chef saw the figure of a man in his car headlights on the drive, walking towards the front door of the house, as he was leaving to go home. The man disappeared when the chef stopped to ask his identity. According to Underwood, the chef described him as wearing a top hat and long overcoat with a short cape. The same figure was also seen at the main gates to the house in daylight a few weeks later. The man, described as tall and wearing a top hat and cloak by the staff member who saw and sketched him, was also seen at the reception desk by the company secretary when he was leaving the building late in the evening after a long day working. He was horrified to see the figure sitting at the desk with his head tipped back, as if he was laughing. An all-pervading chill went through him and he rushed out to his waiting taxi. His subsequent drawing, so Fox contends, is very similar to that of the earlier drawing, made after the daylight sighting.

The ghostly shape of a woman was seen in one of the attic bedrooms and was reported by the owners of the house when it was a country club. They also reported sightings of a coach and four horses driving at speed up the drive.

The 'ashen' face of a young man with staring eyes was seen from the pantry window by the caretaker's son after he and his father were alerted to intruders at the premises by their dog's barking. After thoroughly searching the perimeter of the house, they had found that, although the back door was shaking violently, it had not opened and was still locked and intact. The pantry was in the oldest part of the house and through the metal mesh over the window the young man's appearance considerably startled the caretaker's son. Investigation showed that the pantry was padlocked and no one was inside.

J.P. Chilcott-Monk tells us that for nearly 200 years the cook and the murderer keep what he calls a 'ghostly rendezvous' each December and that the coachman, if such he be, is more likely to show himself on a Wednesday if this falls on the twentieth of the month.

Testwood House today.

The junction between Salisbury Road and Cook's Lane, where the body from Testwood House was dumped.

Peter Underwood reported that in 1965 the Ghost Club, of which he was president for many years, visited Testwood House. An atmosphere he described as 'waiting' was remarked on by several of the members. The back door, he made sure to note, did not rattle…

The Anchor Inn

David Hart joined a group from Haunted Southampton Ltd in their investigation at the Anchor Inn in Redbridge. He took a series of three photographs of the bar, all taken within fifteen seconds. They are reproduced in this book, as they have been the cause of much discussion since he began to show them to friends.

'It was half past one or two o'clock in the morning,' he says. My wife Briony and I were the only ones in the room. There was a mirror behind the bar area and we took the camera there. I normally take two photographs but this time I took three.'

In the mirror in the first picture two people can be discerned, David and Briony; the second shot only shows David; the third shot appears to show a figure in a black coat or cloak. There were only two people in the room, one in a white top and the other in a rugby top.

'We used a Ouija Board that night and we supposedly spoke to two people, French sailors from the Second World War period. They were French but speaking English. I now associate the image in the third photograph with the big coats or macs used on the fishing boats.'

The photographer and his wife can be seen in the mirror. (Photograph courtesy of David Hart)

In this picture the photographer stands alone. (Photograph courtesy of David Hart)

Has he been joined by a ghostly sailor in black? (Photograph courtesy of Dave Hart)

Some of David's friends have suggested that they can see a face on the wooden panelling on the front of the bar. He cannot see this but enough people have said it to make him pause. The image remains to be explained.

Juliet and Pete Collins, of Haunted Southampton Ltd, explain what happened to them at this pub. Juliet reveals:

It was the first time I had picked up a video camera. We went down into the cellar in the Anchor public house in Redbridge, opposite the old medieval bridge. It was a small room, apparently much bigger originally but it had all been built in. We sat there, there were things from Christmas on shelves, I put my torch down on the desk. It was just a small one with a fabric carry handle. I picked up the camera and said 'Let's go for it'. We were there five minutes! The only light source was the night vision camera and it suddenly flooded with light and I turned around and realised that the torch had come on by itself. We didn't know what to say so thanked the spirit and asked if he could turn it off again. It started flickering. It got dimmer and flickered and eventually went out. It was brilliant. Then we said, 'Bet you can't turn it on again.' Ping! Then I said, 'Go on, turn if off again.' Ping again. That was four times without touching it.

Pete continues:

That is evidence. We have the video and it has had about 30,000 hits on YouTube. There is a priest hole there, so it must be old. The ghost is said to be, so the previous owners thought, a chap called Boysy Russell. His family used to own the pub in 1912 and when he was seventeen he went on the *Titanic*. He did not return. The previous owner said they were always hearing footsteps upstairs. They were the only people in the pub. That is why they thought the place was haunted. They thought it was Boysy Russell coming back. We spent the whole night there and found so much information about the place – we went to the archives in the civic centre and in Winchester – it was fascinating.

The Red Lion Public House

The Red Lion, in the High Street, is a bit of a mish-mash of time periods. The cellar dates from 1148, when the Normans ruled England, parts of the main building date from the Tudor era and, inside, some of the building dates back to the 1950s. It was here that the famous 'Southampton Plot' treason trial was held against three conspirators, Richard, Earl of Cambridge, Lord Scrope of Masham and Sir Thomas Grey of Heton, who plotted the death of Henry V in 1415. They wished to replace Henry with Edmund Mortimer, fifth Earl of March. The horrified Mortimer rushed straight to the king when he heard of the plot. The room known as the 'Court Room' in the pub, where the trial was held, is half-timbered. The three were found guilty and were executed at the city's Bargate.

The Red Lion has its share of ghosts, including a procession of mournful people leading from the pub to the Bargate, which is just a few hundred yards away. Paranormal investigators have visited the pub before and found evidence of ghostly activity. The most commonly sighted apparition is of a lady in her sixties, who drifts through the bar area.

Haunted Southampton Ltd have been to the Red Lion several times. Kelly Leigh and Lee Davies were two of those who spent the night there, experiencing what the spirits at the pub had to offer.

'We went down into the cellar,' says Kelly. 'I felt sick. The psychic artist with us turned and ran, saying she too felt sick.'

'You walk through a little tiny door and you have to duck your head because it is very low. We went down ten steps, which were quite steep. Down there you can hear people moving about and the floor creaking,' Lee says. Kelly then continues:

> We went to the back part of the cellar, with the wall in between. All of a sudden we heard the door open, and we heard someone coming down the stairs. Their footsteps were quite heavy, like chunky boots. I said "Quick, let's hide! It's spooky!"

Note the large orb on the beam inside the Red Lion. (Photograph courtesy of Merita King)

I heard the steps and then dived, thinking this is really wicked, we can't scare them. It was pitch black. I just thought I can't do that.

'It soon backfired,' says Lee ruefully. 'Kelly looked around the corner and said, "Lee, there's nobody there."' Kelly goes on:

The door was closed at the top. I thought someone was going to do the same to us as we were to them – jump out on us, so I was going along with my torch saying 'It's alright, you can come out now. Fun's over. Please don't jump out on me and make me scream.' I was talking but there was no one there. We tried walking down the stairs to see if we could make the sounds we had heard, but our feet didn't make the same noise. It was like someone in a suit of armour coming down.

The historic Red Lion pub.

2

Netley

Netley Abbey

Just along the road from the Royal Victoria Country Park lie the picturesque ruins of the Abbey of St Mary of Edwardstowe, otherwise known as Netley Abbey. The last Hampshire monastery to be established, it was founded in 1238 as a Cistercian Abbey by Peter des Roches (died 9 June 1238), the Bishop of Winchester under King John and later, Henry III. The first monks to occupy the abbey came from Beaulieu and were engaged in sheep farming and forestry.

The abbey had the reputation for assisting travellers. This was not surprising as it was situated so close to Southampton Water. It suffered under Henry VIII, when the

The stately ruins of Netley Abbey.

Dissolution of the Monasteries led to it becoming a private house and the home of the Lord Treasurer, Sir William Paulet. He destroyed much of the building in his wish to make it a grand home. It was further sacked in the seventeenth century when much of the fabric of the building was sold off to Southampton builder Walter Taylor, who was building houses in the area, in particular on the Isle of Wight.

Taylor, so we understand from word of mouth through the centuries, was worried about a vivid dream he had had. In it, a falling keystone from one of the abbey windows killed him. So concerned was he about this dream that he confided it to a friend, Isaac Watts, the father of the celebrated hymn writer, Dr Isaac Watts (1674 – 1748), and asked for advice. Watts thought the dream was a sign of God's displeasure at the desecration of the site and counselled Taylor to have no further business with the demolition. Sadly, greed got the better of Mr Taylor and he decided to carry on with dismantling the abbey building. Disaster soon struck, when the keystone of a window arch fell from its place and hit Taylor's head, fracturing his skull. He died shortly afterwards. As a consequence, no further demolition work was undertaken at the site and so we have the dramatic ruin that is Netley today.

The story of Blind Peter adds richness to the abbey's store of legends. He is said to have been the keeper of the abbey's treasure at the Dissolution of the Monasteries, and hid the treasure to avoid it being seized by Henry VIII's men. His white, habit-clad figure is said to haunt the abbey cloisters on Halloween. The treasure was never found. A treasure seeker, one Mr Slown, is said to have tried to find the haunted hoard. Soon after he began to dig in a hopeful spot, something so frightened him that he ran from

Walter Taylor's greed in demolishing the abbey for its stone, led to his demise.

the site screaming and collapsed, dying. His last words, according to the Southern Life website, were: 'For God's sake, block it up.'

Ian Fox, in the *Haunted Places of Hampshire*, comments on the feeling many women get at the abbot's lodging, a place that has had many reports of strange, hazy shapes drifting aimlessly within and around it. The feeling is of evil and the reports, all saying the same thing, are numerous.

Fox also tells of the 1991 event experienced by David Breeze and his wife, the custodian of the site for English Heritage, whose house is to one side of the abbey grounds, with a direct view of the ruins. The story goes that when Mrs Breeze was putting their child to bed, she caught sight of a 'small, glowing light' on top of the building. Mr Breeze fetched his dog and the pair went to see what the light was. The light was in the high triforium, the raised gallery above the nave, and was the size of a football, sitting stationary in the air. The light, described as 'giving off an orange-red incandescence' slowly faded away as Mr Breeze watched it. He could not find any explanation for the phenomenon, which did not seem to affect his dog in any way.

Other tales concerning Netley Abbey tell of a lady dressed in white, with a parasol, who is sometimes seen walking across the abbey lawns, and of a motorist, whose car engine stopped outside the abbey grounds on the road just as he saw two nebulous shapes drifting towards the abbey. When they had passed, the engine started again.

Netley Abbey is open to the public and makes a peaceful spot for a picnic. Just remember though, you may be sharing it with unseen others!

The Ghosts at Netley

Netley, the little village a stone's throw from Southampton on Southampton Water, is a quiet place, with a row of colourful terraced houses facing the waves. It is easy to see the village of yesteryear in the twenty-first century streets, despite the cars that speed through it now.

A terrace of Netley homes.

It was in Netley that the Royal Military Hospital was built, at a cost of £350,000. It opened in 1866 and at the time it was thought to be the biggest military hospital in the world, being so large that postmen used bicycles to travel along its quarter-mile long interior corridors to deliver their letters.

Florence Nightingale had severely criticised the design of the hospital as out of date and, looking at surviving photographs, it is easy to see why. Corridors were long and eerie, despite the magnificent windows which gave fine views of the waterside. Wards were badly ventilated and gloomy, with no natural light. There was little scope to increase capacity in times of war, when casualties would be expected to arrive in their hundreds.

The hospital took casualties from the Boer War, and both World Wars. Florence was right, casualties had to be packed wherever they could find space and huts soon sprang up in the grounds for the overflow and for staff accommodation. Netley later became a military psychiatric hospital and the little cemetery, to one side of the main site, has a section that is looked after by the Commonwealth War Graves Commission.

Ian Fox, in *The Haunted Places of Hampshire*, tells his readers that the existence of a ghost at Netley was treated almost like a 'military secret'. The hospital's staff were told not to discuss the repeated sightings of the apparition of a Grey Lady. By ignoring it, it did not exist, or so the top brass sought to insist. This apparition usually appeared, and was followed shortly afterwards, by the death of the patient by whose bedside she stood.

This photograph, taken just before the Royal Military Hospital was demolished, shows just how eerie the corridors could be. (Photograph courtesy of the Lingwood Netley Hospital Archive)

An orb in the Royal Victoria Country Park. (Photograph courtesy of Merita King)

The Netley Grey Lady was said, by Peter Underwood in *The A-Z of British Ghosts*, to have been a Crimean War nurse, dressed in a blue-grey uniform. Fox cites Stephen Darby in the early twentieth century, who investigated the sightings and uncovered the fact that a nursing sister had leapt to her death from the upper part of the building after she had killed her lover, a Netley Hospital patient, by poisoning him. She had found him with his arms around another woman and green-eyed jealousy had reared its ugly head. There are several versions of this story. One has her accidentally giving her patient an overdose and another has her committing suicide, unable to live without her lover after his death. Underwood mentions the possibility that the apparition might have been Florence Nightingale herself, trying to stop the hospital from being closed.

The Grey Lady was most often seen downstairs in the main corridor, or her skirts were heard rustling as she walked by, leaving a strong perfumed scent to the air behind her.

There was an exorcism service held at the hospital in 1951, but the sightings continued after this time.

The hospital main building, apart from the chapel, was demolished in 1966, after many years of disuse. The last known sighting of the Grey Lady was reported by the demolition contractor, who saw her at a ward entrance. It would seem that she was continuing her nursing duties right to the end.

The Netley Hospital grounds are now home to the Royal Victoria Country Park and are open to the public for recreation. One visitor was Merita King, a local medium, who went there with a friend after dark one night. The pair hoped to see some sign of paranormal activity in the area and took along a camera to try to record what they saw.

What is this? It was not visible to the naked eye and only appeared in one of Merita King's photographs, taken in the grounds of the Royal Victoria Country Park. If you look closely, you can see the trees and grass through the image. (Photograph courtesy of Merita King)

Merita takes up the story:

'We were walking and we had gone all the way to the cemetery, around the cemetery and we were walking back. I was explaining to my friend how disappointed I was that we had not really got much [to show for the walk] and we were taking photographs as we went.'

One of the photographs that Merita took was part of a series she shot by standing on the spot and turning 360 degrees, clicking the shutter each time as she turned. All the other photographs showed a peaceful woodland scene at night, except one, which clearly showed a misty image. She says:

> That is the whole photo. It has not been cropped or retouched in any way. You can actually see the grass and the trees and what not. It was a fairly chilly night but it was not chilly enough to see your breath. We weren't smoking and I swore when I saw it. It was the most incredible thing! The pictures either side of it were completely blank and neither of us could see this mist with the naked eye. It is the best mist shot I have ever taken. People say that it looks like a horrible mouth, or like John Merrick, the elephant man.

The mist is unexplained.

Abbey Hall, Netley

At first glance, the community hall in Netley village hardly looks to be a place of much interest. It looks to be exactly what it is – a 1990s-built village hall, open as a place for locals to hold events when they need to hire a venue. Yet, according to the Southern Paranormal UK website, it has been worthy of two investigations by the group.

In July 2009 nine members gathered, led by Julie Harwood, Southern Paranormal's creator and leader, to investigate the hall once again. They had experienced strange, unexplained noises in the entrance hall to the building and the team had had a pen lid thrown at them on the last visit. They wanted to see if there was anything further happening there and were joined by the Abbey Hall caretaker.

The Abbey Hall was built on the site of the old Jubilee Hall. It is situated on the ancient waterside, close to Netley Abbey and just up the road from the Royal Victoria Country Park, the site of the old Royal Military Hospital. It sits therefore, amidst an area rich in reports of ghostly sightings and the Abbey Hall has been the subject of what the website calls a 'blessing/clearance', 'to put people's minds at rest'.

The investigators formed small teams that each held vigils at various parts of the building – the foyer and kitchen, the main hall, and the backstage corridor and the area under the stage.

The results, which were filmed and properly recorded, were startling. Light anomalies, or orbs, were seen in various parts of the building and one was filmed by camcorder travelling over the keys of a keyboard situated under the stage. Cameras

Abbey Hall, Netley.

It seems hard to imagine in this 1890 Victoria Road, Netley, shot, that the village is the subject of so many ghostly sightings. (Photograph courtesy of Julie Green)

were seen to move by themselves and the recorded pictures show that the camera was being moved up, defying gravity, and down again. Despite the storm that was lashing down outside, and taking the sound of this into account, the team could not explain several of the noises they heard at the various vigil points. These ranged from audible groans to bangs and thumps. One of the trigger objects, a key, placed on the stage, had moved two centimetres. Other members of the team reported hearing a child laugh and experiencing a sudden chill in parts of the Abbey Hall.

The medium with the team reported seeing the dark shadow of a man walk out of one wall and got the impression of a man who was constantly working, whilst being disabled in some way, with a back or leg problem.

The results, only part of which are recorded here, paint a picture of a property that is very active. According to the Southern Paranormal website, the group would like to continue their investigations at this venue in the future.

3

Further Afield

The Swanwick Ghost

The website www.trueghosttales.com has kindly allowed the following story to be reproduced. This account comes from Peter McKechnie:

> When I was eighteen I had a girlfriend who lived twenty miles away at Park Gate. To get to and from there I regularly used the train from Cosham to Swanwick Station. To get home on this particular Sunday evening, I arrived at 11pm on Swanwick Station. It is a fairly remote and dingy station and it was unusual for anybody else to be there at this hour, but a lady in

Swanwick Railway Station, scene of an eerie encounter.

her late forties or early fifties was seated waiting for the last train. She was about 5ft 4in tall, of plump build, with permed hair, and was wearing a 'camel' coat and was carrying a very large canvas shopping bag, which had a tartan pattern on it.

I sat down to wait for the train, which were frequently late. After a few minutes the lady asked if there was a train, as she, 'had to get back to Portsmouth'. I told her that I was also waiting for the same train and that it should be along soon. Several times she asked the same question and reinforced that she, 'must get back to Portsmouth'. When the train eventually did arrive, she remained seated but became very agitated and began to cry. I told her that this was the last train, but several times between sobs she repeated, 'I can't go back.' I asked if I could help, and suggested that if she got on the train that perhaps we could talk about any problems she had. But again she said, 'I can't go back.' Meanwhile, the guard had got off of the train to point out that this was the last train on that night and that if I was getting on I should hurry (from his angle he probably couldn't see the lady). Reluctantly I got on the train, and as it pulled out of the station I could see her sobbing.

On the journey home I felt guilty about leaving her, as she was obviously very upset about something. On arriving home at Cosham I telephoned the police at Park Gate and briefly related the story and asked if perhaps somebody could visit the railway station and see if she was OK. I gave a description of her height, dress and the bag she was carrying. I assumed that perhaps some domestic dispute was the cause of her distress.

On arriving home from work the next evening, Monday, my mother drew my attention to an article in the local paper, *The Evening News*. She knew that I caught the train from Swanwick and this article was appealing for witnesses to an accident near that station. I immediately recognized the photograph included in the article as the lady from the previous evening, the description of her clothing, height, dress and bag also matched perfectly. The article was appealing for witnesses to an accident where the lady had been killed whilst walking along the railway lines... on the Saturday evening.

I telephoned the newspaper and suggested that they had confused the dates and that I had spoken to the lady. They checked and to my surprise insisted that the accident had been on Saturday. I then telephoned the police who listened to my story, and indeed confirmed that I had reported the incident on Sunday evening, however were adamant that the incident had occurred on Saturday.

In a subsequent article in the local paper I learned that the lady was called Maureen Hampton, she was a patient in a local mental hospital, Coldeast. She had been allowed out on the Saturday and had been to Portsmouth. Returning in the evening she had missed the station at Swanwick and got off of the train at the next stop, Bursledon. Not being familiar with the area she had decided to walk the short distance back to Swanwick along the lines, and been struck by a train.

Now, I wish I had remained or touched her! However, I caught the bus after this!

(Written by Peter McKechnie for www.TrueGhostTales.com, © 2007)

The Eastleigh Light

One night, during a Second World War air raid, a young man decided to stay in his house in Eastleigh instead of joining his family in the air-raid shelter. He was lying in pitch darkness in his bed, listening to the cacophony of sound outside, when he became aware of a ball of grey light hovering above him. The eerie glow moved towards him and he thought that it could perhaps have been the light from the searchlights or a warden's torch from outside. He soon realised that this was not so, and, hair standing on end, he dived under the bed covers for safety. The man survived the air raid and attributed this to the ghostly ball of light protecting him, just like a guardian angel.

The Brushmakers Arms, Upham

Just six miles outside the very centre of Southampton stands the pretty little village of Upham. In Shoe Lane stands the picturesque Brushmakers Arms public house, run, for the last three years, by Keith Venton, and his wife, Nicola, who live there with their baby son, Alfie, and Keith's son, Kai.

The Brushmakers Arms has a long history of bumps and other phenomena in the night. There was a brush factory down the road from the pub and it is popularly thought that an old, miserly brush salesman, Mr Chickett, stayed there regularly. He was known to keep his money with him and to sleep with it under his pillow at night.

The Brushmakers Arms. (Photograph courtesy of Keith and Nicola Venton)

One morning he was found murdered in his bed; his money was gone. Mr Chickett's ghost has long been associated with the old building and there are numerous accounts of sightings of him as he hunts for his money and his murderer. Keith and Nicola disagree with his reported occupation though:

> We understand that he was the inn keeper or the coach keeper. He had his throat slashed and his money stolen. He was not a brush maker; he was an inn keeper, and a miser. The pub is called the Brushmakers because there was a brush factory up the road. Next door was the bakery and the post office. The cottage now called The School House was the village school apparently. It was a thriving little place. People would not have needed to go very far for anything.

In such a small community Mr Chickett's miserly habits would not have been unknown. However, this is not the only spirit in the old pub. 'The one in the cellar is apparently an old landlord who hung himself, but we don't know the name or anything about that one,' says Keith.

The bedroom in which Mr Chickett is supposed to have met his doom. The wardrobe doors were found open and mirrors cracked. Note the orbs – one particularly noticeable is on the wall between the wardrobes.

Keith had been the chef at the Brushmakers Arms for fifteen years prior to taking over as landlord. At the time, the upper floors were in a state of disrepair and required major renovation. Nicola takes up the story:

When we moved in we had a whole new bathroom put in and the shower ripped out, the old kitchen was pulled out and a new kitchen installed. In one room all the walls were taken back to brick and replastered. In another one the ceiling was horrible, so it got patched up and then we had to replace all the floors. We decorated throughout, so it was major upheaval. The works took about nine months in total and we lived out of one room during this time.

It was during the renovations that Keith and Nicola experienced a series of events that they cannot explain. Nicola continues:

All through that time things would happen. We used to have a little round mirror, almost like a shaving mirror, in Kai's bedroom. It had a crack in it, so I replaced it. Then it was cracked again and I replaced it once more. This happened several times and each time there was a crack in the same place – straight through the mirror – so, in the end, I gave up. The wardrobe doors in Kai's bedroom kept being opened too. We have two big wardrobes with heavy doors and we were down in the bar one evening and we could hear really loud banging. It sounded like something was fallen over, like a unit. I went upstairs and all the wardrobe doors were open in the bedroom.

When Kai was nine or ten, we had lived here for six or eight months, he came out of the bedroom in the middle of the night. I was in the front room and he said to me, 'Oh, who's burning something?' He was half asleep. I said, 'What do you mean?' He said, 'I can smell burning. It's disgusting. It's making me feel sick.' I thought it was the kitchen downstairs, so I quickly went down but found nothing, the kitchen was finished, it was ten or eleven o'clock at night. I went back into his room and I said, 'Come on, I'll come with you and put you to bed.' He kept saying, 'Can't you smell it? It's horrible.' I could not smell anything in the room. I got the air freshener and sprayed it all the way through and asked him if that was better. He said, 'Oh yes, much better,' and went straight back to bed. We have now put smoke alarms all over the building.

It is believed that Kai's bedroom, the largest room at the front of the building, was the room in which Mr Chickett met his grisly end.

I have a tiny cat ornament, which sits covering a scratch on a shelf upstairs. On the front of the cat it says, 'No home is complete without a cat'. Every morning I would find it facing the wall. It's as if it had been naughty. I was convinced it was Keith and he was winding me up and so I stayed up one night until he had gone to bed, so I knew the cat was in the right position. I got up in the morning and it was turned around. Our spirit did not like the cat ornament.

It was never malicious things that happened; it was more pranks and tricks. Keith would put his cheque book down on the table and then accuse me of moving it. We would hunt high and low thinking we didn't want it to fall in the wrong hands. Three weeks later it would be on the dining room table, where it had been. We pulled the place apart looking for it, but it would turn up in the place he said he had last had it.

The ghost in the living room at the Brushmakers Arms does not like the little cat ornament sitting on the shelf just inside the door!

We had two cats when we moved in here. I was convinced that the older one, Gilbert, saw things. Once, I was sitting in the front room on the sofa on my own and he was outside the lounge door. He would not come in. He was a lap cat and wouldn't leave me alone, so this was unusual. He was growling. Keith picked him up, told him to stop being silly, and carried him into the front room. Gilbert was staring next to me, not looking at me but at a spot next to me. Keith put him down on the sofa and Gilbert went wild. He scratched my arms trying to get away and he ran out of the room back to where he had been. He wouldn't come in to the front room.

One of the weirdest things was when we were woken up by what sounded like a wild animal in the front room. I quickly got up and turned the light on and both the cats were cowering in the corner with big bushy tails. I managed to settle them down and went back to bed. Keith got up in the morning and went to the office, then came back to me in the bedroom. 'Were you up playing with all the money last night?' he asked me. 'No, I was not,' I replied. I explained about the cats in the night and how I calmed them down. 'Come and look at this,' he replied. I went into the office and all the money was piled up. All the pound coins, and the notes – all the fifties, the twenties, the tens – were all sorted out. 'That was not me!' I said. 'I would not get up at two in the morning and get all the money out. If I did I would have at least counted it and left a total for you!'

Gilbert had a fit once. I found him on the floor. We rushed him to the vet and they said they thought he was frightened. That was after the incident when he scratched me and he went wild. I am convinced he saw something.

There are at least eight orbs in this photograph of the kitchen in the Brushmakers Arms. The floor was spotless – that large circle is an orb!

My friend has a little girl. When we first moved in she was two and they both came to visit. We were all in the front room. The little girl wandered off and then we were worried that she would go near the stairs so my friend said she would go and get her. We found her by herself in the kitchen. My friend asked her daughter what she was doing. She said, 'Oh, I'm just talking to the little girl.' We said, 'Oh, right sweetheart, come with us,' and took her away. There was no one else in the room at all.

Keith added:

When I worked here as the chef I used to get changed upstairs. I was upstairs one day when, all of a sudden, one of the big fire doors swung open and then closed. I looked for the landlord, Tony, but he was in the cellar. There wasn't anyone else who could have opened the door.

For ages there was a spate of losing the torch on my Wednesday night off. We have a little black torch and the staff use it to let themselves out when they have locked up and turned

A former landlord hung himself in the cellar at the Brushmakers Arms. Now he helps the present landlord move his empty barrels about.

the lights off. Whoever locks up would open the door, turn around, put the torch on the table by the back door and then go. I could never find the torch in the morning on a Thursday. It would be on the fire, on the fireplace, on the window sill…

'Then there was the time we had some girls in here, having a meal around the table. Two of them were local and two from further away,' says Nicola. 'I was sitting at the side of the bar and all of a sudden the stereo came on in the kitchen. It had been switched off and unplugged. I went and had a look to check.'

Keith continues:

Another night a couple of locals were here and it came on again. That time we could hear a barrel being scrapped across the floor in the cellar. I had put an empty barrel inside the door, which needed to go to the cellar hatch. I had not done it yet. When I looked, there the barrel was at the cellar hatch! People have accused us of making up the stories just to keep the myth alive. I have better things to do with my time than that.

Most of the events experienced at the Brushmakers Arms happened when the renovations were on-going. However, in the same week that the Ventons spoke to the author for this book, they were disturbed by strange happenings in their baby son Alfie's room, which seem to be a continuation of events that happened when they moved him into his own nursery. Nicola says:

Alfie sleeps from half past seven in the evening through to half past six the next morning. At four o'clock in the morning on 25 April 2010, when I was about to go back to work after maternity leave, the mobile above his cot came on. [Alfie has a large, colourful, musical, revolving mobile suspended above his cot.] We have a baby monitor, and I woke up and I could hear music. Oh my god, I thought, what's going on, the baby's rolled over and hit the button. He sleeps at one end of the cot and the on/off button is way out of his reach. I leapt up, bounced to his room, flung open the door and came running in – he was fast asleep but the mobile was just going round, playing. So I turned it off and crept back out and it was fine. He slept through until half past seven but something set the mobile off. I had tripped in my haste to get to him, broke my big toe and ended up in hospital the next day. I went to work on crutches!

A couple of times recently, while we have been having renovations done to the toilets downstairs, things have happened. When there is a noise the baby monitor, alerts us – it has lights that light up so the noisier it is the more lights there are. On Tuesday this week, the lights were lighting up like crazy but there was no noise. I woke up, said to Keith that there's something wrong with the baby monitor and he said, 'No, there's nothing.' Then I could hear a scratching and I thought I had shut the cat in the baby's room and he was scratching at the door to get out. So I came running in and checked the room. No cat was in there and nothing was happening. The older cat sometimes hid behind the chair and I thought I had shut the door and obviously he was scratching to get out. The cat was in the front room, though, and Alfie was fast asleep. I went back to bed. An hour later and the monitor was on again. The lights were flashing and I came back in to Alfie's room. He was asleep and there was no noise in there, so I could not understand it.

The nursery at the
Brushmakers Arms.

I was completely sceptical until we moved here. Within the first few days of living here people kept saying, 'Oh, it's got ghosts!' and I said, 'Yeah, yeah, whatever!' I didn't think anything of it and then funny things started to happen.

The Ventons were happy for photographs to be taken upstairs at the Brushmakers Arms. The photographs taken in the kitchen and in Kai's bedroom both showed orbs, the kitchen showing several. There may be rational explanations as to the various events that have been experienced here, but, it is hard to think of them in the face of so many first-hand stories.

The Braishfield Ghost

The ladies from the Women's Institute, in their informative and comprehensive book, *It Happened in Hampshire*, written in 1937 about the miserly lady who lived in this little village a few miles north of Southampton.

Apparently, she lived in fear that her considerable wealth would be forcibly stolen from her and so she found an unnamed and isolated cottage in the village, and hid her cash there, under the yew tree in the garden. Shortly afterwards, she died. Since that time, reports of sightings of her abound and she is heard frequently, knocking at the cottage door,(identified by Wendy Boase as the Windmill Cottage in Dark Lane) and making strange noises. The cottage owners, apparently, have got used to her presence and ignore her. She is also reported to frequent the yew tree and dogs, sensing her presence, often stop and growl when walking past. It is thought that she is trying to alert her heirs to the presence of her lost treasure.

Hythe and District Cottage Hospital

Hythe Hospital, the ninety-year-old cottage hospital, which temporarily closed its doors to patients amidst an infection scare in early 2010, is a war memorial like no other.

Doreen Eley, in her foreword to Pam Whittington's hugely interesting history, *Hythe Hospital: A War Memorial Remembered*, which details the history of this popular medical establishment, tells us of the Dibden War Memorial (Hythe is part of the Parish of Dibden): 'It was a courageous and imaginative decision to commemorate those who died on active service for their country by providing a cottage hospital for the needs of the living.' The decision to build the hospital as a war memorial to the men who lost their lives in the First World War, was taken in 1919. The hospital opened in 1922 in Atheling Road and moved to the White House in 1940.

Hythe Hospital, a war memorial.

The White House, Hythe Cottage Hospital.

As with so many hospitals, the Hythe Cottage Hospital has a ghost. Her name, so legend has it, is Minnie, and she was a maid who had been employed by the former owners of the White House. The story says that she had been 'wronged' by the family's son and, when she learnt that he wanted nothing further to do with her, in despair, she went into the garden and plunged to her death by flinging herself down the property's well.

Minnie made herself known to the matron in the 1950s. Miss Harby listed such unexplained events as lights and taps being turned on and off for no apparent reason, and crockery and trays falling from tables, when they were securely sited and no one was nearby. A patient reported the figure of an unknown lady walking away down a corridor at this time. The figure was never identified.

When Miss Davis arrived at the hospital to work as a nurse in 1959 – she was to become matron years later – she mentioned that outside one of the doors, and in one particular corridor that she described as 'eerie', she always experienced the sensation of the hair on the back of her neck rising. She could never account for this frisson of fear.

Night duty nurses often reported hearing an unexplained swishing sound and experiencing the movement of air, as if someone was walking by. This was never explained.

The well was filled in and Minnie's appearances grew scarce, but, in the early 1980s, a patient asked a nurse for the name of the young lady who was standing with her. The nurse was completely unaware of anyone beside her, but the patient described a girl in a cap and apron – a maid's uniform.

Tanglewood

Sharron Baddams has lived at her home, Tanglewood, in Twiggs Lane, Marchwood, since July 2007. The house is a 1960s-built bungalow, built on woodland. 'The house is along a route used by highwaymen, according to local stories,' she says, 'and there is a tree just up the lane called the 'Hanging Tree', where highwaymen were said to be hung.' The house was formerly the site from which the local foxhunt left. 'I have experienced quite a few things here.' She continues:

> In the living room some small, heart-shaped, Wedgewood trinket boxes that were left to me by my late nan have moved from where I put them. A substantial, floral painting that was securely fixed to the wall, and had been there since we moved in, fell off the wall and sheared a plug socket off. It was on the wall next to the cabinet that the trinket boxes are on. DVDs placed on top of the TV have flown off.
>
> In the kitchen a pond pump placed right back against the wall at the back of my sideboard, which is about 20in deep, fell off right in front of my husband and I, as we sat at the kitchen table. It wasn't broken by the fall, even though the kitchen floor is tiled and quite a hard surface.

Tanglewood, Marchwood. (Photograph courtesy of Sharron Baddams)

Sharron Baddams saw a man's face at this bedroom window. Exhaustive searching revealed no trace of an intruder. (Photograph courtesy of Sharron Baddams)

When I was sitting at my kitchen table and everyone was out, the door handle in the utility room was moving as if someone was trying to get in. I was scared because I was on my own in the evening and it was dark outside. I just got up and shut the utility door so I couldn't see it. We don't use that door now; it's always locked. I also see a black shadow out of the corner of my eye whilst in the kitchen.

I had been down at the bottom of my yard to feed my horse and when I looked back at the house I saw a white figure in my hallway. I can only describe it as a shape of a person, but it was next to Nici, my niece who lives here too, and works with me in the office attached to the house, as she walked up the hallway. Nici did not see it.

It is not just Sharron who has experienced strange happenings at the house.

In the hallway Nici has seen a dark shadow of a figure walking past the door reflected in the window of our previous office, which was a spare room in the bungalow, and no one was in the house at the time. It was dark outside, about 4.30 p.m. in wintertime, and the window acted a bit like a mirror. In the bathroom, the sinks taps turned on three times in one day, when both Nici and I were in the bungalow. We blamed each other for leaving them on, but we are sure we didn't. My bedroom appeared to have a face looking out of the window, which we saw from our office window in the old garage. It was so quick but I'm sure it was male and just glanced out of the corner of the bedroom window, looking at us. There was myself, Nici and one of our workmen here at the time and we sent him running into the house to see if it was an intruder, but he found nothing.'

Sharron has investigated the building's history, but has failed to come up with any satisfactory explanation for the strange things that have happened at Tanglewood.

This is not the first time that Sharron and Nici have met with unexplained phenomena.

In our previous house, also in Twiggs Lane, on the other side of the bypass next to the school, called the Old Police House, there was an office already attached to it, which we used as our office. It was always freezing cold in there, even in the summer, which was really strange and Nici hated being left alone in that house. I also saw dark shadows at the bottom of the stairs there.'

Has a spirit moved from the Old Police House to Tanglewood with Sharron and Nici, and in doing so grown in power? It will be interesting to see what happens in the house in the future.

The Dolphin Inn, High Street, Botley

The Dolphin Inn in Botley, just outside Southampton, was once called the Garrison Inn, reflecting its status as a garrison town in days gone by. It dates from the seventeenth century and was a base for Canadian forces during the Second World War.

The Dolphin Inn, which is still a thriving village hostelry, is supposed to be haunted by the spirit of a Civil War Cavalier, nicknamed George by the staff, who is seen now and again in its rooms.

Footsteps outside a bedroom and noises in the cellar have also been heard at the inn. The dining room has a cold spot and there is the feeling of a presence there.

There is also a story that in 1980 the landlady saw something, an 'outline', rushing past her that she said was 'tall and slim'.

4

Ghost Investigators and Mediums Working in Southampton

A Chat with Andrew House

Andrew House, paranormal investigator and a disk jockey on Hedge End's Skyline FM radio station, has been interested in the paranormal since he was a small child:

All my life I've been interested. All my family have been too, so I just kind of went into it as well. My family members were investigators but now it is just me. It was a family thing and I got into it because of them. It has grown from there.

My dad lived in a haunted house in Millbrook, which my aunt still lives in. It is an old council house, which does not surprise me, as traditionally you get poltergeists in council housing. My father experienced a spirit in the night and got quite scared about it, to be honest. It brought up an interest in me to see what causes that kind of phenomena. I have been to the house quite a few times to have a look and it is fairly interesting.

The family have lived there for about thirty years; my granddad owned the house before they did. That's what triggered the interest. The family got involved in visiting haunted places during the day. When I was younger we used to watch the old TV show *Sightings*, and the American programme, *Strange but True*, that kind of thing. I did my first proper investigation when I was twelve – I was quite young.

Hearing Andrew say he undertook his first 'proper' investigation at such a young age prompts the question of just what he means by this:

Before that it was a case of a couple of my friends and I going around to Netley Abbey and Victoria Country Park and places like that during the day and it was interesting. I then got involved with a paranormal group called Haunted Hampshire and I was involved in their investigations. I learnt from other people with more experience and I did a lot of research, reading books and talking to people. When I was sixteen I studied a bit of parapsychology in college in London and from there I continued learning on the job.

When I was sixteen I started my first paranormal group, Paranormal Tours. There are two sides to the business now – the supernatural tours side, which gets the public involved and then the research side, UK PRS, which conducts small, controlled investigations. There are eight of us at UK PRS. We have a lot more control of the environment and this company is for people who want to develop as a parapsychologist or develop as a medium or something along those lines.

So how does an investigation work?

Somebody hears bumps in the night and thinks, Oh crumbs, what's going on here? Southampton Council is a prime example. They have lots of historical places, so much has happened in them. By chance I contacted them, because there was an article in the paper about what was going on, and I had a chat with them. After that, I went around all of their properties to see for myself what was happening at each of them. It was a small, controlled investigation – talking about what had happened at each, interviewing members of staff about it, looking at all the historical places and, after we had done the investigation, we brought in a couple of mediums to see what was going on. We got quite in-depth with the study.

Andrew and his team investigated Westgate, the Bargate, the Vaults, the Merchant's Hall and Tudor House, all ancient buildings within a very small area of the city centre:

The first time we visit a place just a colleague and I go. This is mainly for health and safety reasons, but also to get two versions of the property occupant's account. What we tend to do is to have a chat with them and reassure them, tell them what we can do for them and ask them about their experiences. A lot of people at first are very quiet because they think we think they are a little bit crazy, but then, when we start talking to them, they open up and they say, 'well actually, I've seen this, this and this'. They start to tell us about everything that they have seen. So, we just write it down and probably record it as well. If we think there is something a bit strange going on at that point I would give them a log and ask them, over the next two weeks, to record every single little thing that happens and what time it is, what the temperature is, whether it is cold or hot or whatever, and where it is in the property. There is a reason for this. If it is happening at the same time every day or in the same place every day, then I would start to think that this is maybe a bit logical. It could be what we call a repeater apparition, one that is a bit like an old VCR recorder, I suppose. You record your edition of *X Factor* – no matter how many times you watch that tape it will always be the same. When the conditions are right the repeat apparition will be the same every time. So that is why we ask people to record times and things like that. We also ask them to record who is involved, because with poltergeists they sometimes centre on a person, as opposed to a property. They tend to be people who are going through changes in their life. Traditionally, it tends to be girls or people who have depression or stress or something like that. They tend to get poltergeists around them because they are hormonal and have body changes, so you have to look at those kinds of things. So you look at logical factors before you look at paranormal factors. I think that is quite an important thing to do, otherwise you would be saying it was a ghost and it might not be. If, after the two-week log, you start to see something a little bit odd, then we would say to the occupants, 'OK, what we will do is spend the night here, have a few experiments and we will bring a medium around as well.

We have had investigations before where people have said that they don't want to be there, they just want to know what is happening, which is fine. We had someone like this about two years ago in Portsmouth. The man who lived there was about 6ft tall and he was a security guard. He would not be in the house when we were talking about it, as he was that scared. So, for people to be that frightened there must be something going on, even if it is not paranormal. You do get a lot of cases where it is natural but you have to be careful how you say that to someone.

You go to a lot of places and the occupants really, really want them to be haunted and sometimes that can be a bad thing. The person wants it to be a ghost so much whereas it might be the building cooling down on a hot summer's day or something like that. The odd places you go to are public places whose owners don't want it to be haunted because it can put off the customers! They don't want the exposure to the media that they will have if they find out a place is haunted. It's fifty-fifty really. Private places like it for publicity and it makes them interesting. Those who believe in spirits probably do want the occurrences to be paranormal. But it is very varied.

Listening to Andrew, it seems easy to understand how normal, everyday events can be interpreted as out of the ordinary. For this reason he takes each case based on its own merits. He does not jump to hasty decisions, rather he works logically through the evidence before coming to a conclusion. The importance of this methodology should not be underestimated.

Haunted Southampton Ltd

Juliet and Pete Collins run the overnight paranormal investigative company Haunted Southampton Ltd in their spare time.

'From knee high to a grasshopper I was always reading ghost stories, ghost and sci-fi films and stuff like that,' says Juliet. She elaborates:

Most Haunted started on television about eight or nine years ago, and of course, I was instantly into that. I used to sit there and watch it and Pete would be outside talking to his brother. He actually sat down and watched it once with me, it happened to be a particularly good episode, and he was hooked! He has been more and more interested as time goes on. Now the kids are getting older we have more free time to be able to go out in the evening. At least we can trust them not to burn the house down now!

About five years ago, I went on a ghost walk with my sister on the Isle of Wight, we went around Newport with Mark Tuckey, who does a lot on the island. It was fascinating. I then dragged Pete on one down at St Catherine's, at the lighthouse.

Then we went to an event there and Mark was talking about vigils that he had done. I thought I would love to do this and gave him my telephone number. He phoned me about a year after that and said that he was doing a ghost hunt in the Prince of Wales, a pub I used to go to when I was a lass. It is just outside Osborne House. I said 'Yes' and we, and Pete's brother and his girlfriend, spent the night in a haunted pub. That was our first vigil. We spent about an hour and three quarters in the loft laughing. It was the first time we had ever done an 'Is there anybody there' type thing and I think the first time anybody does it, as far as I can tell, they all have a bit of a giggle. After that, we were hooked. We did some more investigations, including one at Arreton Manor, but we thought the medium there was a bit strange. He was saying that people were channelling spirits when it was really just an optical illusion and so I said, 'No!' We left. The trigger object moved though, so there was something going on.

'It was the way it was run and the way it was set up,' says Pete. He continues:

There was no information afterwards, no feedback and no discussion of what went on. Everybody just said 'bye' and left. Obviously it was a way to make money and there is nothing wrong with that at all, but we did not like the medium. We saw him at three events and he had a routine, between him and the people attending. It undermines credibility.

We sat down and talked about it and the more we talked the more animated we got about it. Like that guy on the island, we have no qualifications as paranormal investigators. Why couldn't we do something like that? Surely, we thought, if we put our savings into it and get some equipment for people to use if they want to, and try to coax a medium to come along, we could put on a night that encompasses not only old, traditional Ouija Board techniques, calling out and dowsing rods, but also things like EVP (Electronic Voice Phenomenon) monitors and modern stuff. So we phoned up people and asked if they would be interested in a ghost hunt and received lots of rejections – 'No, thanks. Bye.' I used to do telephone sales years ago before I became a nurse, so I did not give up and I found someone who was interested. We trawled the internet – The Red Lion in Boldre was our first one. What a night. It was very exciting. We sat down at the end of the evening and asked 'What did you find?' 'What happened to you?' 'Did you hear or see anything?' Then we tried to research the place. We are not historians either, but we think it only fair if we can actually say, well, that name is… It could possibly be this person. It gives validation to their efforts. It makes them think, wow! Perhaps we really did talk to somebody. I can't say yes or no definitely whether there are spirits and hauntings, but a lot of funny things happen that you can't explain away.'

Some people go to the Haunted Southampton events hoping to hear from loved ones. Juliet explains:

I hate giving people false hope. Making something seem what it isn't or lying to people is not what it is all about. I really hate that. We are just there to see what happens and to report. We put our reports online. I am way behind on them, but never mind, I'm trying! I do try and make pains to say, if nothing happened, nothing happened. If letters on the Ouija Board didn't make any sense, they didn't make any sense.

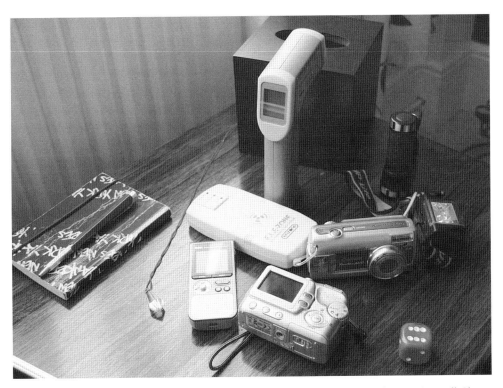

Rob Butler's ghost investigation kit. Note the large, red dice, which spirits liked to play with at No. 2 Romill Close.

Haunted Southampton have carried out investigations at various points in its year-long history and now numbers over 1,000 'friends' on its Facebook site.

Kit — Gadgets to Take on Investigations

Rob Butler takes a metal briefcase to the investigations he attends with Southern Paranormal UK. In it are some essential items of kit that he uses during his enquiries.

The large red dice, from his step-daughter's giant snakes and ladders set, is something he uses as a trigger object. 'It seems to have some significance,' he says. 'If it is a child spirit that I am picking up on in an investigation, they may like to play with the dice. I take it with me.'

He also takes along a voice recorder, a camera, a head torch, an EMF (Electromagnetic Field) monitor, a police right-angled torch and a digital thermometer. 'The EMF meter changes colour when spirits walk in front of it — it goes yellow or red on the display — and if there is a cold spot that is when you use the digital thermometer.' Rob also carries a Swiss army knife 'just in case' and notepaper with a pen he can use in the dark.

'Screwdrivers, batteries, crystals and my dowsing rods are in my other case,' he says. 'I don't always take them with me.'

It would seem that, in addition to being interested in the paranormal, the average investigator needs a strong arm to carry his kit, too!

Merita King

Merita King is a down-to-earth, pleasant lady who lives in Bishopstoke. She is also a medium. I asked Merita what this actually entails.

'It means I communicate with those in the spirit world, basically, in one sentence, that is what it is. I communicate with the spirit world.'

Merita King.

Mediumistic ability is not always something that just happens overnight. However, in Merita's case, she has always known that she might have some kind of tendency in that direction.

She says:

I think the ability is always there. I did not actively work to bring it to the fore until I was about forty I suppose, because when it's the right time, it happens. But I have always known that that is what I have wanted to do. I tried many times to start the journey myself but never got anywhere, and when you try something if it is not the right time, you won't succeed. When it was the right time, it just happened. So it's as though I have always been a medium, although I had to wait until whomever, the universe, if you like, decided right, now, is the moment.

I suppose my upbringing helped a lot. My dad was a medium. So I knew right from an early age that the spirit world was there and I was brought up with an understanding of it and an acceptance of it – it's part of normal existence.

I have also been told that a couple of generations back, on my mother's side, there was a medium, my great-grandmother, who had the ability but did not use it, she chose not to. I think really there has to be something like that – not so much to hand the ability down but to give the child the awareness of it. They can choose to explore if they want. I knew it was something that I wanted to do – to explore further – I always knew that.

I used to buy books, I used to pump people for information, I used to go along to meetings and workshops and buy packs of tarot cards – anything that popped up I would have a go at but it never went anywhere beyond the first couple of tentative steps and I got so frustrated with it, I just thought, sod it and just went back to normal daily life. And then, quite by chance, it just crept back on its own. The opportunities were there and nothing stood in my way.

The first thing that happened was that I started going out with this chap who was into the spirit world, and it came up in conversation quite a lot. He knew some other people who were also very interested, so the conversation was around the subject a lot of the time. He used to do things like meditation and so I started trying meditation and that got the old desire going again. Then, when we broke up, I came to live here and I remembered having seen a sign in Eastleigh for a spiritualist church. So I went down to Eastleigh to have a look but the sign had gone. There was no sign of the church there and so I just took it as yet another vain attempt. I carried on trying my own meditation, just sitting down quietly and breathing, and continued buying books. After about a year, I found out that there was a church again in Eastleigh in that same place. I did not realise that the hurricane in 1987 had damaged the building and they had had to pull it down and rebuild it. So, I went there; just turned up and said, 'Can I come in?' That is when I met the people who were able to help me learn how to develop properly and start focusing.

I looked to them as people who had already done what I wanted to do. I was a bit naïve. I thought that everyone in the spiritualist church would automatically know everything about it. I did not realise that people who go there do not know everything and don't always want to explore. I went a few times and got nattering to people and I asked about how one goes about developing as a medium. They said that I needed to sit in the circle and that is how it started. I joined their open circle.

I was in there for two or three years. An open circle is where you can just turn up and join in. It is for beginners and then, when the people who run it feel you are ready, they invite you to join the closed circle. So that is the circle I am in now. I have been in the closed circle for four or five years, I suppose.

You are expected to have a certain amount of experience of working in your mediumship and it is also taken for granted that you want to develop it further in the closed circle. Being as it is in the church, they do encourage you to actually use your mediumship there, but they do not force you to. Not all of us want to. I don't particularly want to just stand up in church every week and be a medium in church. Some do and that's fine. The closed circle is people who seriously want to develop. It is not really for someone who just wants to have a bash and see what it's all about. It is taken for granted that you have a certain commitment and you've made the decision to dedicate quite a bit of your focus to mediumship.

You develop it by using it. You sit there and you learn all about deep meditation. What you have to do when you want to communicate with a spirit is to switch off from the physical world and just move to the side a little bit. You have to close off your awareness as much as you can, to allow the more subtle awareness of the spiritual energetic side to come in. It is so subtle it is drowned out as soon as you start focusing your mind on something physical – if it is too powerful, it shuts it off. You learn to switch off and switch on like that, like retuning a radio – that is the way we often illustrate it – just like retuning a radio. The signal is quite a weak one and the stronger one keeps trying to interfere but you have to ignore that and keep focused on the weak little signal. The scientific part of it is that the human body creates electricity inside and we know, it has been scientifically proven, that we have an electrical field around us, which we call the Aura. Everything on the planet is vibrating at different wavelengths and when you are being very physically engaged, and physically focused, your wavelength will be at a certain level. Communicating with spirit involves a very different kind of a wavelength. You have to adjust your own towards this optimum interactive level, where your mind can communicate. But also, those in the spirit world can alter theirs too, to come down to us. We have to meet in the middle.

This all sounds very involved but there may a danger that even if you have mastered the technique to communication, there may be no spirit there to communicate with. Merita says:

You can be the most powerful medium in the world but if the spirit does not want to talk to you, you will get nothing. We cannot summon them or force them to come. It is up to them whether they choose to come and talk to us or not and they have to work just as hard to achieve that communication as we do. That is why quite often we will give a reading to someone and they will not be able to take some of it. It is a very tenuous link. We are having to step aside from the fact that we are based in a very physically dense place, and they are working very hard as well, and a lot of the things that come through come through symbolically and can be quite subtle. We can misinterpret what we are feeling, or seeing or hearing. It is so easy to get it wrong. We are not one hundred per cent all the time, much as we would love to be.

It is a constant process. You never learn all there is to know. You never reach the end of your development processes. The way you work changes, the way spirits work with you changes, and you will have different guides working with you from time to time. You will have new challenges. When, for example, I first started realising that I was getting comfortable and confident with my mediumship, and I was able to start giving readings and felt I was giving evidence that people could accept, I used to always just see the images that were given to me. Or I would have a sense of just knowing – we call it claircognisance. Recently, within the past year, I actually started hearing a lot more and I hear a lot now. You do not hear it as a voice. You are left thinking that you hear a voice but it is not like that. You hear it as a thought. but you know it is not yours because it feels different and it sounds different. It is often totally unconnected with what you were thinking about. It's a bit difficult to describe but it happens, you know it straight away. It's quite interesting and once you start working with it and accepting it, it's going to get stronger. If you ignore it or don't trust it, or if you think, well I'm going to be a right prune if this is wrong, it never develops. You have to actually speak.

Merita, in common with many mediums, has spirit guides who have chosen to work with her:

They make the choice to work with you, to help you with a particular area of your life. You'll have some that are with you throughout your life and you will have others who come and go for a specific thing. Some of them are there just for moral or emotional support. You'll have family members around because they have an emotional bond and they still want to know what's going on with your life and they want to be a part of that. You will also have other ones who aren't family members and who are there to steer you along your chosen path. They will do things like make sure you get the right opportunity at the right time and make sure you don't take the roads you are not supposed to take. They are the ones who will allow you to get into a spot of bother here and there because you have to learn how to get out of it.

I have a Native American guide who has been with me for many years and it is only since I actually found out who he was that I realised certain things that happened when I was much younger were little ways of him showing himself. For instance, my grandmother collected Beswick horses. She lived in Alton and in her dining room she had corner shelves, right up high. She had a Beswick horse on each of them. I remember being four years old and when we used to visit her I used to ask if I could go and look at the one on the top shelf. She would say yes, and she would come and stand in the dining room – I wasn't allowed anywhere near it, I was just allowed to stand and look. And I knew, I even remembered what it felt like, and I knew it was important. I didn't know why. I just knew there was some importance to it. It is only now, since I realised I have a Native American spirit guide, that I understand he must have been there all the time and it was his presence that was giving me that tiny little bit of awareness. His name was Tatanka Okanka – Buffalo Laying Down, almost the name that the whites gave him. The whites could not translate their language completely correctly because they did not have a written language at that time. When he used to sign his name he would draw this picture of a buffalo lying down. That was another reason why he was called Sitting Bull.

It was a weird thing that cemented his identity for me, because I am somebody who is a bit sceptical about things. When people say I have so and so as a guide, if it is someone

I have heard of I tend to automatically think, yeah, they're a nutter! I know a Native American man who does drum healing, and I used to go along to his group in Emsworth. On the drive back one night, it was quite late and it was absolutely pouring with rain, I was driving along through Waltham Chase and I was going along by the Fountain. It was pitch black, there wasn't a car for miles behind me or in front of me and yet, when I got to this particular spot, a badger leapt out of the side of the road and jumped right in front of my car. I missed him by inches! I didn't dare to stamp on the brakes because if I had… it was pouring with rain. There was all that space and he waited for me. It wasn't until months later, when I was researching my guide, I found out that when he was a small child he was called 'Jumping Badger' and when I read that I nearly fell off my chair. That was a spooky moment!

Merita now uses her mediumship to give readings to people over the telephone, by email and face to face. As her confidence has grown, so have her abilities. She also now sometimes aids investigative teams with their enquiries into haunted properties.

Ross Bartlett – The Youngest British Medium

Ross Bartlett is a likeable young man with an old head on his shoulders. In fact, when you talk to him, you realise very quickly that he not only loves what he does for a living, but feels that he has a gift that it is his duty to share with others. This maturity in one who is not long past his eighteenth birthday, and who is the youngest medium in Britain today, is startling when first encountered.

Ross lives in the Banister Park area of Southampton and tries to work as often as possible in and around the city. He says:

I do a lot of work here. I started off working in Southampton. The spiritualist church is in my local area and I do my private readings based in Southampton; two different evenings a week in and around the local vicinity. I do demonstrations in the area, in Hill Lane and The Avenue, at the spiritualist church and a club there. I do demonstrations at the Concord Club in Eastleigh too. I started here and began to spread out, into different areas, and got the opportunity to do a bit of work abroad, which was nice, but I definitely want to stay here, close to my roots. I don't travel to do private readings, I just do them all here and people come to me. It is easier that way and I just go out and do the public demonstrations elsewhere.

This paints a picture of a busy person, so how did it all begin?

It probably all started off when I learned I had the gift, when I was about five or six years of age. I had my first clairvoyant vision when I was in my mother's bedroom. I was lying on the bed and I saw a figure of a lady just come up to the bed and lean over me. She had a long flowing dress on, there was a brooch to the left side of her, her hair was done up in a bonnet

Ross Bartlett, Britain's youngest medium.

and she was in her fifties or sixties. She sort of disappeared, vanished, after that. That was the first experience I had.

You might think I'd be scared or freaked out, but when you are a child like that you are not afraid of much at all, are you? It was all just a new experience. It was fresh. It was quite a calming. I felt secure with the fact that there was someone there, watching over me, and there was somebody in the room with me at the time. Yet, it was just an experience. Now I look upon it as being a lot different to how I saw it then. Spirits continued [to visit me] around that point.

I mentioned it to my grandmother at the time and she thought it could have been a very close friend who she thought of as being an aunt. She had lived next door and often visited our home and watched over the family, when they were going through bad times.

These incidents continued after that. I would see things and I would hear odd things, like my name being called out or sounds like people whispering. As I got older, certainly round about nine or ten, more physical experiences were starting to happen, like when a glass was on a kitchen side, in a row with about six or seven others, and one glass in the middle came out of the row and started travelling along the table. I was still very young but my grandmother was there at the time, washing up, as you do – it was just a normal day really – and she came around and caught the glass. She waited until it stopped, picked it up and put it back, and got on with her washing up! I stared in complete astonishment. She said, 'Oh, things just happen like that sometimes.' So as a kid, you just get on with it, don't you?

I do believe that my grandmother was aware of these sorts of things. She died when I was quite young, so we never really got the chance to have a proper, in-depth conversation about everything. She was always very much a religious lady, and I think she was just comfortable whatever happened.

In addition to attending spiritualist churches in the area and practicing his gift, Ross took a course at the Arthur Findlay College for the Advancement of Spiritualism and Psychic Sciences, in Stansted Mountfitchet, in Essex, when he was sixteen. He is widely read and is fascinated by the scientific side of mediumship, particularly quantum physics and the spirit world, the afterlife and communication between this world and the next:

I study hypnotherapy and hypnosis as well, which is all the mind and body connection and psychological forces. I know a lot about the spiritual side of things, so I kind of have that whole mesh and that is quite rare I find. Not a lot of people are able to say, 'Yeah, I can do this,' or, 'There is an afterlife.' They won't psychically be able to explain fact, and science is really starting to catch up with it and explain what most, if not all, mystics, enlightened people throughout time, prophets have been saying in different ways, and it is fascinating.

At the Arthur Findlay College Ross was able to learn from some of the older generation of mediums:

I grew up, luckily enough, to experience different levels of physical phenomena but not to the extent that they have. I am very interested and they intrigued me further. I find that knowledge and understanding helps you in every walk of life. If you look at it you can understand how you perform better and exactly how you do the things you do. Then you can adapt it and better your way of doing it.

When I started out I wasn't bad. [Ross laughs as he says this.] But I was nowhere near the level I am now. I developed very quickly because the ability was there, waiting to burst out.

Ross is a mental medium, 'Which,' he says, 'is how I make my living and what I have become known for.' A mental medium is one who is able to relay verbally information received by mental telepathy within his consciousness. According to the very informative website, www.monstrous.com, which has a useful set of definitions for those new to the terms used in spiritualism, a mental medium 'hears, sees and feels what the spirit communicators are relating'. It is then the medium's function to relay this information to the sitter.

Ross goes on:

I have a set number of people in the spirit world that help me do what I do. The most common term would probably be guides, but it is a phrase I dislike because it is coined all over the place. They are just regular people.

The way mediumship works is that I can't read myself, and I can't give readings of myself and communicate with my grandmother, because I don't know how much my own mind is coming into it. It's the same with the guides. I can sense they are there but, because I don't know how much my own mind might be coming into play, I choose to keep a fence, a boundary if you like. I know where they are and that they are helping me, but I don't want to know too much about them. It is fine that they do their job and I love them for it, but I don't want to delve in any deeper at this stage because I try to stay as grounded as possible. Part of my job is dealing with people from all sorts of different backgrounds and all sorts of different jobs. They won't be able to connect if I start going off about this or that guide and they would not listen as much. The point would not get across. That is not what it is about. Mental mediumship is about proving the existence of life after life, personal to you, your relatives, wherever I'm reading, and you don't do that by giving somebody a guide or an angel. You have to prove it to them, which is something that has grown with time, as I have got better. As I have got better the evidence has got better. I try to be as direct as possible. I look upon it as being a performance and I have to try to do better each time. When I started off I gave names and things but now I will go straight to a person in the audience and go on from there, by being much more direct and as evidential as possible. I can give road names, addresses and numbers. To be able to get that sort of evidence, and the memory links, personality descriptions, and physical descriptions, is important. People like it because it is something that you could not know. If I came to you and named your grandfather, you would know immediately and I would be proving my point.

Is it possible to contact a spirit every time of trying? Ross replies:

Well, I have been asked this quite a bit. It has never happened that I have to give someone a reading and I have nothing. I would be in a mess if it happened. Every person's reading will be slightly different for many reasons. The spirit coming through will change how the reading goes slightly, depending on their character. And also the energy and the place and the room make a difference. I could go to somebody and give them a whole load of evidence, everything is right, names and whatever; it might be their grandfather's link in the army, or their father's. With the next person, the reading will go a lot slower, or maybe I won't give as much evidence. I will still try and get that contact across. I will start the reading with that person's first name or the condition they passed with. Sure, it can't be done every time, I'm just human and I am not infallible.

It's all about keeping the right balance in life so you are at your best. If I drank and I had a hangover and I had to do a demonstration, it would not go well. There are lots of important steps. I do a meditation process before I give anybody a reading, which takes about twenty minutes to do it comfortably. You can rush it but, you know, I prefer not to and that is just getting myself into the right frame of mind and focus to be able to do it and give off evidence. When I am not doing that I'm just regular me.

Ross is engaged to Emily, who works at the John Lewis department store in Southampton. 'I spend a lot of time with her,' says Ross. 'Emily is very supportive. She comes along to all my demonstrations.'

Does Ross worry about losing his mediumistic abilities, his 'gift' as he believes it to be? This question brings a long pause to the conversation as he ponders his response. It is the first quiet spell for some time:

I think my gift is a natural ability that everybody has to a certain degree; that everyone can tap into. We can all kick a football but we are not all David Beckham. Some people can start off naturally playing football better than others. I just think it is the same for mediumship. Most of us have had some sort of experience in our life where we have thought what was that? That is just your intuition. Everyone has, we are all the same. Our bodies are just matter, which is energy condensed to a low vibrational state, and we all have roughly the same genetic makeup and the same sort of mind, so it stands to reason that we all have the same ability, gift, whatever you want to call it, to a certain degree. For that reason I am not really scared to lose it. I could deteriorate, and not be as good as I was or am now perhaps. If I did not practice and then I went back to doing it, I would not be as potent. But I am not really worried about losing it.

Being the youngest medium in the country carries quite a responsibility. 'I don't think about it too much,' he says. 'Yes, I am the youngest medium in the UK and I will be probably for quite a time still. I literally left school and went into it straight away. So, for somebody to actually do it younger than that they would have to leave school early, you know.'

So where does Ross think he will be in ten years time? This question holds no problems for him and he answers instantly.

I want to go with the flow over the next few years. I have certain goals that I would like to achieve – more TV work, as you can reach the most people like that. I also think the Internet is going to be very useful in the future and I want to think about projects involving those two together, the TV and the Internet. I am also interested in physical mediumship. I am trying to get things together and go down that avenue, and give people some insight and experiences in that regard. That is amazing stuff. If you can produce on film for somebody a full materialisation, they will not be able to doubt you.

Ross Bartlett is a medium to watch!

Joan Shergold

I spoke to Joan Shergold about how she first knew she had a psychic gift:

> I was recovering from surgery. I was stretched out on the settee and there was a writing pad
> and pencil on the table for me to make notes. It was 1980 and I was watching *Pot Black*. All
> of a sudden, I picked up the pen with my right hand (I am left handed) and I started to make
> lines on the paper. I still have that drawing, in my album. I thought, well, that's interesting,
> because I was drawing a line coming down to the point and stopping with my right hand.
> I thought, I can't do that! Now I can do it because I have been doing it for years. Then I
> started doing sharp lines, to see where they stopped and always they stopped at the point.

Joan is a matter-of-fact lady who believes in fate. 'Everything happens for a purpose,'
she says. 'Up until I started drawing psychically, I was always drawing, I was an artist
already.' In 1981, Joan took a photograph of Aphrodite's Pool in Cyprus and then painted
a picture of it from the photo. 'The point is, when people look at it, they say, 'Who is that
sitting on the side?' I did not paint anyone sitting on the side, I just painted the rock. It
came out looking like that. It just happens. When it happens, I don't question anything.'

For several years Joan was a regular artist medium at several of the spiritualist
churches in Southampton. She drew at both the church meetings and at home. One of
the drawings she is most interested in is one she drew on 1 April 2005, All Fools' Day.
The picture, of a jolly-looking man in costume reminiscent of the Tudor period or of
royalty in robes, has her baffled.

Joan Shergold's painting – is it a rock or a spirit in the bottom right-hand corner?

Do you recognise this man? Joan Shergold would love to know who he is.

Whenever she draws, Joan makes sure that the picture has a full history with it, giving details of her impressions and any information she receives from the spirit as she draws.

This picture is reproduced in this book in the hope that someone may recognise him. 'Because of the way in which I worked as an artist medium, I have one or two unclaimed drawings. One in particular I have never shown to the public. It is of a bearded gentleman wearing "royal" or state clothes and a coronet. The date, 1 April, is very significant,' she says.

The caption on the drawing reads:

The first thing brought to my attention is a red velvet pudding-basin cap trimmed with white fur. The personality is good, sort of jovial and as the drawing progressed showing a beard, there was a chuckle when I remarked, 'You look like a jolly Father Christmas!' The colouring could be white or in life a light ginger-brown.

Shown by the ear is the gift of Clair-audience [being able to hear voices]. He is a good listener, too. In the material area of life is shown a lady wearing a flat hat tied down with a veil. There is a miniature silhouette portrait of the same lady on the upper lip. I suggest this lady makes her presence felt through her perfume.

A book of Religious content is shown lying on a table.

There is an indication of a very extrovert life-style; drinking maybe and possible womanizing.

As this drawing was completed on 1st April one can be aware it may concern a joke – perhaps fancy-dress.

While Joan was talking about this spirit she became aware that he was with her at that moment, and that he quite liked the author, busy looking at his picture. It would seem that once a flirt, always a flirt!

As an artist, medium Joan has had some funny experiences:

I never looked at them [the people in the spiritualist church] because I could very easily do a likeness of you and say it is your grandfather. One of the funniest times I ever had though was when I drew a bearded gentleman and this man at the back of the church said, 'Oh, look! Oh, you are with me!'

'Are you sure, can you take all the things I have said?' I replied.

'Yes.'

'Who is it then?' I asked.

He said, 'You've drawn Jesus Christ for me!'

I said, 'No, I haven't!'

'Yes, you have! He's my spirit guide, you've drawn Jesus Christ for me and he's my guide.'

'No, I haven't done that,' I said. 'I am not saying that the gentleman doesn't come from the same era, because he certainly does look like someone from then and I'm not saying he is not with you, but I am saying he is not Jesus Christ.'

He said, 'He is, I know he is.'

I said, 'I know he isn't. I'm telling you if I had drawn Jesus Christ and I knew he was Jesus Christ then I would keep him and I certainly wouldn't be giving him away.'

'Oh!' was the man's reply!

I had a very strange experience walking down the road. There was a woman over the road, walking towards me, and I looked at her and thought, good heavens! That is my sister. My sister is dead but it was my sister walking down the road towards me. Funny, I thought, I must cross over and talk to her and so I did. I went up to the woman and I said, 'We don't know each other do we?' and she said, 'No, we don't.' 'No,' I replied, 'but I have to tell you, I really thought you were my sister walking towards me.' She said, 'But that is funny, because I thought you were my sister walking towards me! But I do see her on people.' 'Yes, I know what you mean,' I replied and left it at that. It was walking up Warwick Road. My sister overshadowed her and her sister overshadowed me. She was probably a medium too but we did not exchange that sort of information.

Joan tells the story of how she took an acquaintance to her own funeral. This sounds completely bizarre, except for the fact that her recital of the ghost story comes across with quiet dignity and so is completely believable.

Joan first met Nelly Blatcher when she and her husband Ron were asked to give her a lift to the Golden Wedding celebrations for Joan's friend, Mrs Westley, Nelly's sister. Nelly had been a bridesmaid at the wedding all those years before and did not want to be late to the party now. She was very impatient. 'I can't think why they didn't send a special car for me. If I had known you would go so slow, I would have taken a taxi,' Joan says Nelly somewhat ungratefully told the couple. She continued:

Nelly continued to get more and more distraught until, in the end, I turned round and told the old lady quite firmly, 'Sit back and keep quiet please. You will not be late. In fact you will get there at exactly the right time! Others might be late, but not you.' Surprised by my tone she sat back for the rest of the journey, talking about the wedding fifty years earlier, and only occasionally firing vitriolic darts about being late at her very patient driver, my husband.

It was a happy party, full of reunions with old friends, including Nelly's son, Ron. We didn't stay to the end and someone else took Nelly home. That was five months ago and she didn't come to my attention again until two weeks ago.

A chance meeting with Mrs Westley told me that 'poor Nelly' was in hospital, very ill with a terminal condition. It was only a matter of time and they were trying to get hold of her son, Ron. I left her with such words of comfort as I could muster and decided to watch the local paper for an announcement of the death and funeral, which I would attend if possible.

There was no news of this kind but one morning a little later I awoke without any anticipation of special events. I was tidying the bedroom at ten o'clock when I had a sudden compulsion to dress myself in outdoor wear and visit Mrs Westley. It seemed urgently important to know how Nelly was getting on.

At eleven thirty I pulled up outside the Westleys' home in Spring Road, in Sholing, and was startled to see the curtains drawn, both upstairs and down. It was unusual because Mrs Westley is a meticulously careful and house-proud woman. I sat for a moment wondering what to do and then clearly I heard it:

'We'll be late! We'll be late!'

The realisation was immediate, the reason for the drawn curtains and the tangible distress emanating from the seat behind me. Nelly had died and that day was her funeral. But I did not know where or what time it was scheduled to be.

Again I heard, 'We'll be late! We'll be late!' I started to drive. Although I observed the rules of the road, I didn't notice which way I was going. I was only aware of the persuasive presence at my back, directing my movements and willing me to go faster. It required all my effort to resist until suddenly I remembered something, stopped the car and half turned to look at the apparently empty seat behind me.

'Nelly,' I said firmly, 'Will you sit back and keep quiet please. You will not be late. You will arrive at exactly the right time. Others might be late, but not you!'

There seemed to be a definite easing of pressure from the back seat as I started up again to continue the journey. Eventually I saw a road sign to the City Crematorium and entered its gates. It was twelve, noon, exactly. I turned towards the back seat again.

'There you go Nelly,' I said cheerfully, 'I can't do anymore. Someone will take care of you, I'm sure.' There was a moment as if of hesitation and then I was alone. It was a normal day again and I was able to go home.

When I passed Mrs Westley's house on a later occasion, I went in. She was very tearful about what a trying day it had been.

I told her that I had been to the crematorium, but that I did not know when the funeral would be. I asked her why she hadn't let me know about it.

'Ronnie wouldn't have any notices printed. He said no one would be interested in his mother's funeral, except family. You went to the crematorium? That's where it was, but how did you know she had died?'

'Never mind about that,' I said. 'Just tell me one thing – were you late for the funeral?'

'Mrs Westley told me that the funeral had been arranged for twelve o'clock, noon, and at a quarter to the hearse hadn't arrived, although the undertaker had said it would be a good half hour journey. 'Our Nelly would not have stood for that if she'd been there. Really strong on punctuality she was.' I didn't like to tell her that Nelly hadn't been late and I had taken her to her own funeral.

Bibliography

Books

Beddington, W.G. and Christy, E.B. Eds., *It Happened in Hampshire* (The Hampshire Federation of Women's Institutes, 1936)

Chilcott-Monk. J.P., *Ghosts of South Hampshire and Beyond* (G.F. Wilson and Co. Ltd, 1980)

Hapgood, S., *500 British Ghosts and Hauntings* (Foulsham, 1993)

Parr, D.A., *Ghosts of Hampshire and the Isle of Wight: Web of Fear* (The Breedon Books Publishing Co. 1996)

Sandell, E.M., *Southampton Cavalcade* (G.F. Wilson & Co. Ltd, 1953)

Underwood, P., *The A-Z of British Ghosts* (Chancellor Press, 1992)

Whittington, P., *Hythe Hospital, a war memorial remembered* (Itchen Printers Ltd, 1991)

Articles

Hamilton, K., 'Unwelcome visitors whose call brings terror' (*Daily Echo*, undated)

Kennedy, R., 'It's farewell to the famous Blue Star' (*Evening Chronicle*, 2003)

Websites

www.artvaults.org.uk
www.arthurfindlaycollege.org
www.bbc.co.uk
www.braishfield.org
www.ewingssolicitors.co.uk
www.ghosts.monstrous.com
www.mysteriousbritain.co.uk
www.teenpsychic.co.uk
www.southampton.gov.uk
www.southernlife.org.uk
www.southernparanormal.com
www.trueghosttales.com
www.ukparanormal.moonfruit.co.uk
www.vrsouthampton.co.uk
www.wikipedia.org

Other titles published by The History Press

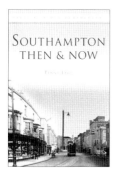

Southampton Then & Now
PENNY LEGG

The major port city of Southampton has a rich heritage, which is uniquely reflected in this fascinating new compilation. Contrasting a selection of eighty-nine archive images with full-colour modern photographs, this book reveals the ever-changing face of Southampton. Inspiring fond memories in many, and revealing the Southampton of yesteryear to others, this volume will appeal to all who know and love the ever-changing city.

978 0 7524 5693 5

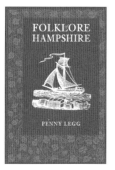

Folklore of Hampshire
PENNY LEGG

Folklore of Hampshire explores the rich heritage of the county's traditions, seasonal customs, saints' lore, hill figures, holy wells and songs. The county is proud host to traditions and legends that may seem strange to residents of Hampshire in the twenty-first century, but which were very real to the Hampshire folk of yesteryear. Richly illustrated, this book explores the origins and meanings of county traditions to create a sense of how the customs of the past have influenced the ways of the present.

978 0 7524 5179 4

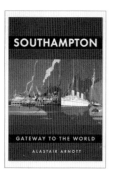

Southampton: Gateway to the World
ALASTAIR ARNOTT

The history of Southampton is tied to its maritime heritage. This book explores the intimate relationship the city has with its near neighbour the sea, tracing its development throughout the centuries. Written by a former Southampton museum curator, this book provides expert insight into the history of shipping, traditionally the city's most prominent industry, which has allowed it to become known as the 'Gateway to the World'.

978 0 7524 5357 6

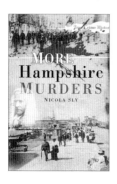

More Hampshire Murders
NICOLA SLY

In this follow-up to *Hampshire Murders*, Nicola Sly brings together more murderous tales from across the county. They include the last recorded fatal duel to have been fought in England in 1845, the mysterious death of Andover businessman William Parsons in 1858, and the 1888 killing of Annie Vaughan. Nicola Sly's well-illustrated and enthralling text will appeal to everyone interested in true crime and the shady side of Hampshire's history.

978 0 7524 5495 5

Visit our website and discover thousands of other History Press books.

www.thehistorypress.co.uk